Darya Malyutina

MIGRANT FRIENDSHIPS IN A SUPER-DIVERSE CITY

Russian-Speakers and their Social Relationships in London in the 21st Century

With a foreword by Claire Dwyer

ibidem-Verlag
Stuttgart

Bibliografische Information der Deutschen Nationalbibliothek
Die Deutsche Nationalbibliothek verzeichnet diese Publikation in der Deutschen Nationalbibliografie; detaillierte bibliografische Daten sind im Internet über http://dnb.d-nb.de abrufbar.

Bibliographic information published by the Deutsche Nationalbibliothek
Die Deutsche Nationalbibliothek lists this publication in the Deutsche Nationalbibliografie; detailed bibliographic data are available in the Internet at http://dnb.d-nb.de.

∞

Gedruckt auf alterungsbeständigem, säurefreien Papier
Printed on acid-free paper

ISSN: 1614-3515

ISBN-13: 978-3-8382-0652-3

© *ibidem*-Verlag
Stuttgart 2015

Alle Rechte vorbehalten

Das Werk einschließlich aller seiner Teile ist urheberrechtlich geschützt. Jede Verwertung außerhalb der engen Grenzen des Urheberrechtsgesetzes ist ohne Zustimmung des Verlages unzulässig und strafbar. Dies gilt insbesondere für Vervielfältigungen, Übersetzungen, Mikroverfilmungen und elektronische Speicherformen sowie die Einspeicherung und Verarbeitung in elektronischen Systemen.

All rights reserved. No part of this publication may be reproduced, stored in or introduced into a retrieval system, or transmitted, in any form, or by any means (electronic, mechanical, photocopying, recording or otherwise) without the prior written permission of the publisher. Any person who does any unauthorized act in relation to this publication may be liable to criminal prosecution and civil claims for damages.

Printed in the EU

Soviet and Post-Soviet Politics and Society (SPPS) Vol. 148
ISSN 1614-3515

General Editor: Andreas Umland,
Institute for Euro-Atlantic Cooperation, Kyiv, umland@stanfordalumni.org

Commissioning Editor: Max Jakob Horstmann,
London, mjh@ibidem.eu

EDITORIAL COMMITTEE*

DOMESTIC & COMPARATIVE POLITICS
Prof. **Ellen Bos**, *Andrássy University of Budapest*
Dr. **Ingmar Bredies**, *FH Bund, Brühl*
Dr. **Andrey Kazantsev**, *MGIMO (U) MID RF, Moscow*
Prof. **Heiko Pleines**, *University of Bremen*
Prof. **Richard Sakwa**, *University of Kent at Canterbury*
Dr. **Sarah Whitmore**, *Oxford Brookes University*
Dr. **Harald Wydra**, *University of Cambridge*

SOCIETY, CLASS & ETHNICITY
Col. **David Glantz**, *"Journal of Slavic Military Studies"*
Dr. **Marlène Laruelle**, *George Washington University*
Dr. **Stephen Shulman**, *Southern Illinois University*
Prof. **Stefan Troebst**, *University of Leipzig*

POLITICAL ECONOMY & PUBLIC POLICY
Prof. em. **Marshall Goldman**, *Wellesley College, Mass.*
Dr. **Andreas Goldthau**, *Central European University*
Dr. **Robert Kravchuk**, *University of North Carolina*
Dr. **David Lane**, *University of Cambridge*
Dr. **Carol Leonard**, *University of Oxford*
Dr. **Maria Popova**, *McGill University, Montreal*

FOREIGN POLICY & INTERNATIONAL AFFAIRS
Dr. **Peter Duncan**, *University College London*
Dr. **Taras Kuzio**, *Johns Hopkins University*
Prof. **Gerhard Mangott**, *University of Innsbruck*
Dr. **Diana Schmidt-Pfister**, *University of Konstanz*
Dr. **Lisbeth Tarlow**, *Harvard University, Cambridge*
Dr. **Christian Wipperfürth**, *N-Ost Network, Berlin*
Dr. **William Zimmerman**, *University of Michigan*

HISTORY, CULTURE & THOUGHT
Dr. **Catherine Andreyev**, *University of Oxford*
Prof. **Mark Bassin**, *Södertörn University*
Prof. **Karsten Brüggemann**, *Tallinn University*
Dr. **Alexander Etkind**, *University of Cambridge*
Dr. **Gasan Gusejnov**, *Moscow State University*
Prof. em. **Walter Laqueur**, *Georgetown University*
Prof. **Leonid Luks**, *Catholic University of Eichstaett*
Dr. **Olga Malinova**, *Russian Academy of Sciences*
Prof. **Andrei Rogatchevski**, *University of Tromsø*
Dr. **Mark Tauger**, *West Virginia University*
Dr. **Stefan Wiederkehr**, *BBAW, Berlin*

ADVISORY BOARD*

Prof. **Dominique Arel**, *University of Ottawa*
Prof. **Jörg Baberowski**, *Humboldt University of Berlin*
Prof. **Margarita Balmaceda**, *Seton Hall University*
Dr. **John Barber**, *University of Cambridge*
Prof. **Timm Beichelt**, *European University Viadrina*
Dr. **Katrin Boeckh**, *University of Munich*
Prof. em. **Archie Brown**, *University of Oxford*
Dr. **Vyacheslav Bryukhovetsky**, *Kyiv-Mohyla Academy*
Prof. **Timothy Colton**, *Harvard University, Cambridge*
Prof. **Paul D'Anieri**, *University of Florida*
Dr. **Heike Dörrenbächer**, *DGO, Berlin*
Dr. **John Dunlop**, *Hoover Institution, Stanford, California*
Dr. **Sabine Fischer**, *SWP, Berlin*
Dr. **Geir Flikke**, *NUPI, Oslo*
Prof. **David Galbreath**, *University of Aberdeen*
Prof. **Alexander Galkin**, *Russian Academy of Sciences*
Prof. **Frank Golczewski**, *University of Hamburg*
Dr. **Nikolas Gvosdev**, *Naval War College, Newport, RI*
Prof. **Mark von Hagen**, *Arizona State University*
Dr. **Guido Hausmann**, *University of Freiburg i.Br.*
Prof. **Dale Herspring**, *Kansas State University*
Dr. **Stefani Hoffman**, *Hebrew University of Jerusalem*
Prof. **Mikhail Ilyin**, *MGIMO (U) MID RF, Moscow*
Prof. **Vladimir Kantor**, *Higher School of Economics*
Dr. **Ivan Katchanovski**, *University of Ottawa*
Prof. em. **Andrzej Korbonski**, *University of California*
Dr. **Iris Kempe**, *"Caucasus Analytical Digest"*
Prof. **Herbert Küpper**, *Institut für Ostrecht Regensburg*
Dr. **Rainer Lindner**, *CEEER, Berlin*
Dr. **Vladimir Malakhov**, *Russian Academy of Sciences*

Dr. **Luke March**, *University of Edinburgh*
Prof. **Michael McFaul**, *US Embassy at Moscow*
Prof. **Birgit Menzel**, *University of Mainz-Germersheim*
Prof. **Valery Mikhailenko**, *The Urals State University*
Prof. **Emil Pain**, *Higher School of Economics, Moscow*
Dr. **Oleg Podvintsev**, *Russian Academy of Sciences*
Prof. **Olga Popova**, *St. Petersburg State University*
Dr. **Alex Pravda**, *University of Oxford*
Dr. **Erik van Ree**, *University of Amsterdam*
Dr. **Joachim Rogall**, *Robert Bosch Foundation Stuttgart*
Prof. **Peter Rutland**, *Wesleyan University, Middletown*
Prof. **Marat Salikov**, *The Urals State Law Academy*
Dr. **Gwendolyn Sasse**, *University of Oxford*
Prof. **Jutta Scherrer**, *EHESS, Paris*
Prof. **Robert Service**, *University of Oxford*
Mr. **James Sherr**, *RIIA Chatham House London*
Dr. **Oxana Shevel**, *Tufts University, Medford*
Prof. **Eberhard Schneider**, *University of Siegen*
Prof. **Olexander Shnyrkov**, *Shevchenko University, Kyiv*
Prof. **Hans-Henning Schröder**, *SWP, Berlin*
Prof. **Yuri Shapoval**, *Ukrainian Academy of Sciences*
Prof. **Viktor Shnirelman**, *Russian Academy of Sciences*
Dr. **Lisa Sundstrom**, *University of British Columbia*
Dr. **Philip Walters**, *"Religion, State and Society"*, *Oxford*
Prof. **Zenon Wasyliw**, *Ithaca College, New York State*
Dr. **Lucan Way**, *University of Toronto*
Dr. **Markus Wehner**, *"Frankfurter Allgemeine Zeitung"*
Dr. **Andrew Wilson**, *University College London*
Prof. **Jan Zielonka**, *University of Oxford*
Prof. **Andrei Zorin**, *University of Oxford*

* While the Editorial Committee and Advisory Board support the General Editor in the choice and improvement of manuscripts for publication, responsibility for remaining errors and misinterpretations in the series' volumes lies with the books' authors.

Soviet and Post-Soviet Politics and Society (SPPS)
ISSN 1614-3515

Founded in 2004 and refereed since 2007, SPPS makes available affordable English-, German-, and Russian-language studies on the history of the countries of the former Soviet bloc from the late Tsarist period to today. It publishes between 5 and 20 volumes per year and focuses on issues in transitions to and from democracy such as economic crisis, identity formation, civil society development, and constitutional reform in CEE and the NIS. SPPS also aims to highlight so far understudied themes in East European studies such as right-wing radicalism, religious life, higher education, or human rights protection. The authors and titles of all previously published volumes are listed at the end of this book. For a full description of the series and reviews of its books, see
www.ibidem-verlag.de/red/spps.

Editorial correspondence & manuscripts should be sent to: Dr. Andreas Umland, c/o DAAD, German Embassy, vul. Bohdana Khmelnitskoho 25, UA-01901 Kyiv, Ukraine.
e-mail: umland@stanfordalumni.org

Business correspondence & review copy requests should be sent to: *ibidem* Press, Leuschnerstr. 40, 30457 Hannover, Germany; tel.: +49 511 2622200; fax: +49 511 2622201; spps@ibidem.eu.

Authors, reviewers, referees, and editors for (as well as all other persons sympathetic to) SPPS are invited to join its networks at
www.facebook.com/group.php?gid=52638198614
www.linkedin.com/groups?about=&gid=103012
www.xing.com/net/spps-ibidem-verlag/

Recent Volumes

140 René Lenz
Internationalisierung, Kooperation und Transfer
Externe bildungspolitische Akteure in der Russischen Föderation
Mit einem Vorwort von Frank Ettrich
ISBN 978-3-8382-0751-3

141 Juri Plusnin, Yana Zausaeva, Natalia Zhidkevich, Artemy Pozanenko
Wandering Workers
Mores, Behavior, Way of Life, and Political Status of Domestic Russian Labor Migrants
Translated by Julia Kazantseva
ISBN 978-3-8382-0653-0

142 Matthew Kott, David J. Smith (eds.)
Latvia – A Work in Progress?
100 Years of State- and Nation-building
ISBN 978-3-8382-0648-6

143 Инна Чувычкина (ред.)
Экспортные нефте- и газопроводы на постсоветском пространстве
Анализ трубопроводной политики в свете теории международных отношений
ISBN 978-3-8382-0822-0

144 Johann Zajaczkowski
Russland – eine pragmatische Großmacht?
Eine rollentheoretische Untersuchung russischer Außenpolitik am Beispiel der Zusammenarbeit mit den USA nach 9/11 und des Georgienkrieges von 2008
Mit einem Vorwort von Siegfried Schieder
ISBN 978-3-8382-0837-4

145 Boris Popivanov
Changing Images of the Left in Bulgaria
The Challenge of Post-Communism in the Early 21st Century
ISBN 978-3-8382-0667-7

146 Lenka Krátká
A History of the Czechoslovak Ocean Shipping Company 1948-1989
How a Small, Landlocked Country Ran Maritime Business During the Cold War
ISBN 978-3-8382-0666-0

147 Alexander Sergunin
Explaining Russian Foreign Policy Behavior
Theory and Practice
ISBN 978-3-8382-0752-0

Contents

List of tables 7

Acknowledgements 9

Foreword 11

Introduction 15

Chapter 1. Limits of transnationalism 25

    London: a super-diverse city 26
    Russian-speaking migrants in London 30
    Transnationalism: introducing a popular concept in
    migration studies 37
    Who is a transmigrant? 40
    Critique of transnationalism 44
    Conclusions 53

Chapter 2. Ethnicity and social relationships 55

    Ethnicity and migration 56
    Social relationships amongst migrants 60
    The nature of friendship 65
    (post) Soviet friendship 70
    Conclusions 75

Chapter 3. Localising friends 79

    'It just happens' 80
    Looking for Russian-speakers 87
    Expanding networks 89
    Transnational friendships? 92
    Conclusions 97

Chapter 4. Choosing friends — 99

    Degrees of closeness — 99
    Constructing distances among Russian-speakers in the bar — 105
    Divisions within the community — 107
    Affective distancing — 113
    Conclusions — 117

Chapter 5. Rethinking friends — 119

    Becoming cosmopolitan — 119
    Everyday diversity — 124
    Dynamics of change — 127
    Social contexts of cosmopolitanisation — 129
    'Us' and 'Them': questioning the dichotomy — 131
    Ambiguous images of 'otherness' — 133
    Conclusions — 135

Conclusion — 137

Appendix 1: Data on research participants — 143

Bibliography — 145

List of tables

Table 1.1
Post-Soviet population resident in the UK from 2012,
thousands (ONS 2013b) 32

Table 1.2
Main language, 2011 Census (ONS 2013a). 32

Acknowledgements

Thanks to my friends, acquaintances, and colleagues who helped throughout the process of this book's creation.
I am grateful to Alan Latham, James Kneale, Claire Dwyer, and Russell Hitchings for their invaluable academic guidance. Thanks to Tauri Tuvikene for being there to discuss the challenges and quandaries of this research among other things, and sharing good times at UCL while this work was in progress.
Special thanks to all my respondents without whose openness and sometimes even friendship I wouldn't have completed this research.
Thanks to fellow researchers of Russian-speaking migrants for our fruitful discussions: Andy Byford and Olga Bronnikova.
I appreciate the efforts of ibidem-Verlag, especially Andreas Umland and Valerie Lange, who helped make this book physically happen.
I am also grateful to Max Anley for his attentive and sensitive editing of the text.
Thanks to my parents for their support.
Finally, a big thank you goes to Anton Shekhovtsov, for being an important source of motivation and inspiration.

Foreword

Friendships, so integral to everyday social life, have been largely neglected in social science. Perhaps they are so commonplace and so ordinary they have remained invisible in our search for understanding of how social lives are experienced. However, more recently geographers and others have begun to recognise the importance of paying analytical attention to friendship patterns and networks. While most attention has been placed on children's and youth geographies, there has also been a recognition of the significance of friendship in migration studies. As Tim Bunnell *et al.* (2012: 502) have recently argued, a focus on friendship is important in 'unsettling the prevailing emphasis on kin and neighbourhood in seeking to understand the geographies of transnational social life', for, as this study illustrates so well, friendship networks are often the key elements through which contemporary experiences of migration, settlement, and transnational lives can be understood. We have long recognised the role of networks in migration studies—the links which facilitate chains of migration to particular destinations, or the strong bonds which develop between people with shared national backgrounds or migratory experiences in new places. However, we have tended to theorise these networks through the anthropological lens of kin or ethnicity or to prioritise versions of familial networks. This pioneering study brings a fresh analytical insight to the value of studying and analysing friendship networks.

Darya Malyutina's study of Russian-speaking migrants in London puts their friendship networks centre stage. She argues that for this diverse group of young migrants in London tracing their friendships offers the most insight to understanding migration trajectories and contemporary transnational lives. This innovative focus on friendship is based upon an in-depth and insightful qualitative methodological approach which starts not, as previous studies might have done, in an ethnic club or religious organisation, but in a bar. This ethnographic starting point enables Malyutina to then build up a sample of Russian-speaking migrants with whom she builds up trust enabling them to share with her their friendship groups. Malyutina's focus on friendship groups allows her to tease out some of the important conceptual themes which frame her analysis and provide an important critique of the existing limitations of transnational studies of migration.

By tracing the informal friendships which are central to the lives of her informants, Malyutina destabilises some of the confirmed assumptions about the place of ethnicity in migration studies through a nuanced analysis of when and how shared language or national identities matter to her respondents, but also the significance of diverse friendship networks possible within the global city. Indeed, as she illustrates, cosmopolitanism emerges as an important value for her respondents which challenges a reliance on inter-ethnic friendship networks and suggests that wider friendships produce changing dispositions towards ethnic diversity. A focus on friendship networks also provides a much-needed empirical depth to wider work on transnationalism. By analysing the range of friendships which migrants retain, Malyutina is able both to map empirically, and emotionally, how transnational ties are retained and valued alongside an analysis which links the scales of the local and the transnational. Indeed, as she argues, friendship has the 'potential of inspiring and informing mobility'. Her work is important in challenging an assumption of *a priori* transnational or ethnic links, instead using her innovative focus on friendships to establish the importance or insignificance of these links empirically. Her findings are important particularly for migration studies, but they also provide important insights into the ways in which contemporary urban sociality is lived and experienced. This suggests that 'the local' and 'the global' are interlinked in dynamic and sometimes unexpected ways.

This book concentrates on the experiences of a group of migrants to London who have remained largely invisible in migration scholarship and too often caricatured in the popular imagination as either property millionaires or benefit dependents. As Malyutina carefully delineates, Russian-speaking migrants are a significant demographic but cannot be easily defined as a distinct 'ethnic community' and are often simply elided within a pejorative characterisation of 'East Europeans'. This study is therefore particularly important in illuminating the experience of a distinct group of relatively recent, and poorly understood, migrants to London. It also offers significant new directions for future migration research on new migration to 'super-diverse' cities like London which is attentive to diversity and does not rely on narrow framings of either ethnicity or transnationality.

Darya Malyutina has opened up a new strand of migration studies in this book not only in the detailed insights she gives into her own case study of Russian-speaking migrants but also by offering a distinctive approach, through the analysis of friendship networks, for many other scholars of transnationalism and migration.

Claire Dwyer
University College London
July 2015

Introduction

'The milieu is not a refined one, but it is the only one that is acceptable. The Americans are kind, open-hearted, cheerful people, helpful and optimistic, but completely alien. Friendship in the Russian sense with all its violent expressions of emotions, last shirts, quarrels, embraces, and tears is unimaginable here. Everything is based on different rules, on independence, on keeping yourself to yourself, on reserve and self-absorption. The word and the notion "privacy"—that is, in a loose translation, "the private sphere", is for the Americans sacred. It is a coat of armour with which they protect themselves from negative emotions'.

(Dovlatov, S. Private letter cited in Young 2009: 54)

What is the relationship between friendship and migration in the contemporary globalised society and a super-diverse city like London? To what extent do migrants' close informal relationships correspond with commonalities (or differences) of origin, geographic location, cross-border connections, and history of mobility? It would clearly be misleading to say that belonging to a certain 'migrant community' amounts to belonging to a friendship network. Migrants' social relations are not confined to relations between compatriots or migrants only. The constitution of a circle of personal connections and the degrees of personal closeness within that circle depend upon particular personal and structural conditions, as well as the circumstances that lead to migration, its temporal dynamics, and a change in spatial location.

The purpose of this book does not include working out a one-size-fits-all explanation of migrants' friendships. It rather seeks to provide some concrete conclusions and contribute to explorations of the complex role of migrants' friendships. In order to fulfil this aim, I asked myself (and my migrant research subjects) some simple questions: how, when, and why does being a migrant or belonging to the same ethnic or national 'community' matter for being friends with someone? Under which circumstances does it not matter if an individual belongs to a particular 'community' or not? Indeed, can you be friends with someone you call 'completely alien'? Is it possible that 'Russian friendship' may not work with 'others'?

This book is focused on recent Russian-speaking migrants from Russia and other post-Soviet countries living in London. The size of this population has increased since the break-up of the Soviet Union and has grown particularly rapidly since the beginning of the 21st century. Most of my respondents are relatively young, 'middling' migrants (Conradson and Latham 2005a; Knowles and Harper 2009), with a good command of English. Others are employed in low-skilled jobs, albeit not the most low-paid. They are not a particularly visible group in London or in the UK. Contrary to popular perception, most of the Russian-speakers who moved to London within the last 10 to 15 years are neither super-rich mansion-owners nor 'benefit scroungers'. They are 'ordinary' people who exist somewhere in the middle. Indeed, while research on migration is often limited to studies of elites or lower social strata, London's new populations include large numbers of those who live and work in between these extremes. These populations emerged in the process of London's ongoing social, economic, and cultural development as a super-diverse multicultural city.

These groups pose a set of challenges for migration research. They are quite diverse and maintain local and cross-border connectivity in a variety of different ways. Like many researchers of contemporary East European migrants in the UK (Datta 2009; Garapich 2012; Morosanu 2013a; Rabikowska 2010), I was often faced with the occasionally contradictory social ties that migrants maintain with compatriots in London and across borders as well as their contested relationships with non-Russian-speaking Londoners. I found this recently emerged migrant population neither maintains any universal pattern of connectivity nor conforms to abstract notions of a diaspora or a transnational community. Therefore, there was a need to explore the particular social connections of its members in order to find out how migrants' social networks may function, and how they may negotiate their way in a globalised world. I felt that existing explanations were not entirely sufficient. Behind people's words and actions there is something else beyond ethnic solidarity, national identity, cultural background, kinship bonds, neighbourhood connections, unity on the grounds of the common vulnerability of a marginalised minority population, life in an expat 'bubble', or the universal connectivity of border-transcending postnational ties. Migrants' social networks are diverse and dynamic, and the processes that lead to their establishment, sustain them or facilitate their dissolution are a critical but underexplored part of their sociality.

An exploration of these issues provides important insights for theoretical reflections on transnational migration and studies of 'global cities'. Increased mobility and interconnectedness have been addressed in migration literature as significant features of globalisation. 'Global cities' are described as places with the highest concentration of flows of people, ideas, and capital. London in particular has been approached as a city with a socially, culturally, and ethnically diverse population due to enhanced migration, which itself contributes to changes in the social structure, the development of global interconnectedness, and the problematisation of relationships within everyday multiculture. Its super-diversity (Vertovec 2007b), expressed in the increased number of multidimensional differences both between and within new migrant groups in the UK, has also been causing concern in terms of questions of community relations, trust and integration (Vertovec 2010).

London's population has undergone some dynamic changes in the past couple of decades, and the growth of East European migration in particular characterises new trends in its development. While post-accession migrants from East European countries that joined the European Union in the new century have already become an object of voluminous academic research, post-Soviet citizens who identify themselves as Russian-speakers have been the subject of considerably less attention. This book is based on the premise that research into Russian-speakers in London can enhance our current understanding of contemporary urban communities, social ties impacted upon by migration, and the quandaries of living within super-diversity. This research's conceptual framework incorporates thematics that extend beyond a common focus on post-EU accession migrants from Eastern Europe, but draws upon wider migration research perspective, and is attuned to the specific issues which define migrant Russian-speakers' experiences of friendship in super-diverse London.

Theoretically, this book contributes to the understanding of migrant social relationships by conceptualising friendship as manifesting dynamics and differences that retain some ethnic, national, and sociocultural embeddedness, yet cannot be fully accounted for by overarching explanations of kinship and common background. My work thus forms a part of geographical studies of friendship and its role in migration processes that has been developing recently (Bunnell et al. 2012; Conradson and Latham 2005a; Morosanu 2013; Ryan 2011). Friendship was chosen as a conceptual category through which this study could explore the dynamics of routine social interactions, long-term and new attachments, the constitutions of social networks, relationships between compatriots and non-compatriots, and the influence of these factors on migrants' everyday lives in London. The focus on friendship involves concentrating on a relationship between individuals, and avoids the reductive understanding of migrant social ties as existing in isolated ethnic communities. This monograph targets four main themes concerning migration: transnationalism, ethnicity, cosmopolitanisation, and friendship. It contributes to migration studies by stressing the need to pay more attention to the inner diversity of migrant populations, the different structural and personal constraints which affect mobility decisions and future lives as migrants. It advances contemporary scholarship on migration, ethnicity, diversity, social groups and networks by filling in certain gaps in theoretical knowledge and providing much needed empirical evidence to support theoretical conceptualisations.

The first part of this study outlines conceptual approaches to migrant social relations. This part seeks to rethink the ways in which migrants are positioned within the fields of the transnational and the local, the ethnic and the non-ethnic. Chapter 1 suggests a way of looking at contemporary migration that goes beyond the diffuse treatment of transnationalism, where it is understood as the heightened cross-border connectivity resulting from enhanced means of communication and ease of travel. Transnational connectivity implies border-spanning links and interactions between people and institutions that may range from sustaining ties with local communities and families 'back home', the exchange of material resources, travel and communication (Levitt 2001), to political transnationalism, overlapping political memberships, and involvement in home country politics through such means as voting in elections or protest rallies (Bauböck 2003; Van Bochove 2012). Following the works of theorists who claim that with the development of migrant studies the notion of transnationalism is becoming generalised and loosely interpreted (Portes 2001; Smith 2005; Vertovec 1999), I suggest that the concept of transnationalism has to be approached with greater attention to the particular circumstances of migration, and consideration of the stratified and heterogeneous character of contemporary migrant communities. Different migratory situations may challenge and resist the development of postnational (Soysal 1994) or denationalised (Favell 2008) identities and practices. In brief, this chapter summarises scholarly discussion of hyper-connectivity, continuous and overlapping cross-border involvements and belonging, and the proclaimed decrease of national or ethnic affiliations as limited and contingent.

Chapter 2 concentrates on ethnicity and the de-ethnicisation of social ties, and develops ideas of relationships that might be based upon something more nuanced than migrant status and/or mutual ethnic or national affiliation. I draw upon researchers' warnings against taking migrant communities for granted (Bunnell *et al.* 2012; Ryan *et al.* 2008; Wimmer and Glick Schiller 2003). This chapter builds upon demands to critically rethink migrant communities as groups (Brubaker 2004; Eriksen 2002) and focus on the relational aspect of migrant ethnicity, which encompasses the often simultaneous malleability of ethnic boundaries and the rigidity of concerns about the supposedly ethnic determinants of a social group's qualities. Following the developing scholarship on East European migration which aims to distinguish ethnic ties from social connectivity, and critically disentangle the nuanced character of ethnicity as well as the different strengths, uses and values of social ties (Garapich 2012; Morosanu 2013a, 2013b; Ryan 2011), this study positions the idea of migrant sociality as not necessarily ethnic. It demonstrates that, while enhanced mobility does not necessarily lead to denationalisation, migrants should not be approached as groups with demarcated boundaries whose members primarily rely on those who are deemed their co-ethnics in their everyday lives. I emphasise that migrants' relationships may include a much wider set of social ties than just 'ethnic' ones, while excluding connections with those considered to be compatriots and fellow migrants. Drawing upon these ideas, I introduce friendship as an optic for understanding migrant sociality that does not focus merely on transnational connections or ethnic ties. An analysis that concentrates on the actual relationships that people develop, sustain or cut off while living as a migrant can provide insights that inform the patterns of relationships across space and time. Friendship networks are relevant for migration research because they have important affective qualities, are not limited by bonds of kinship or neighbourhood, relatively flexible, and not tied to a given locality. This analysis also considers the sociocultural legacy of late Soviet friendship.

The subsequent three chapters draw upon empirical evidence from a qualitative study of Russian-speaking migrants in London and address the key factors which make friendship relevant for exploring and explaining migrant social connections. Chapter 3 demonstrates how Russian-speakers establish, re-establish and maintain their social networks and friendships while living in London, and how their friendships are connected with place. I discuss what happens when Russian-speakers meet each other in the city, how and why personal contact can be prompted (or not), and how the image of 'Russian friendship' feeds into spatial distances and proximities. This presents a variety of ways in which migrants are connected with each other, and establishes London as a social space where these connections are negotiated and migrants' personal networks are formed.

Chapter 4 focuses on the localised functioning of Russian-speakers' friendship networks in the city, and those factors which limit the development of these ties. Drawing upon the assumption that friendship is perceived as a particular relationship that is negotiated and selectively relied upon by Russian-speaking migrants in the social spaces of London, I develop two premises. First, I demonstrate how friendship becomes one of a range of ways in which people are seen as relating to one another and differentiated by degrees of closeness. Second, the concept of 'ethnic networking' cannot adequately describe the social relationships of migrants who live in conditions of 'super-diversity'. Drawing upon my empirical evidence, I develop Ryan's (2011) arguments in favour of the reappraisal of bonding and bridging ties, incorporating the additional distinctions between friendship and acquaintance noted in Russian studies on friendship (Kharkhordin and Kovaleva 2009), and suggest that it is the characteristics of a relationship such as trust and the perceived affective or pragmatic qualities that migrants rely upon and that have to be considered in an analysis.

Chapter 5 is focused on the ways in which relationships with those considered as 'others' are accorded certain meanings by migrants, and on how attitudes towards different co-inhabitants of diversity are dynamically shaped and re-shaped. The main point of this chapter is that these relationships can be ethnicised and racialised, as well as denationalised and become more cosmopolitan. Indeed, both of these processes intertwine and result in a complex picture of a migrant's positioning of self within the multiculture. Friendship is one of the domains of sociality where these processes are negotiated in practice. I attend here to the patterns of migrants' informal social ties as a domain of cosmopolitanisation and as a development of open and inclusive attitudes in personal relationships. This chapter points to the need for understanding migrant sociality as a complex of informal relationships based upon processes of inclusion and exclusion which are an essential part of migrants' positioning of self in a multicultural city.

In the conclusion, I emphasise that migrants often are not just ethnic communities segregated from the main population and locked into sociality primarily with their compatriots; yet this state of affairs does not necessarily mean that they are therefore highly mobile postnational subjects incorporated into global society. I argue that the location of a migrant group in a city and the dynamics of its development have to be analysed through a range of people's informal relationships in personal networks; these personal networks may be situated in different locations and play an important role in mobility patterns. I argue that friendship should become a more prominent theme in research on migrant communities. It is a relationship which is not limited by more fixed kinship or neighbourhood ties (Ryan *et al.* 2008; Wellman *et al.* 1988), has significant potential in inspiring and sustaining mobility (Conradson and Latham 2005a), and is a specific affective relationship irreducible to ethnic or national solidarity (Bunnell *et al.* 2012; Morosanu 2013a). I conclude by outlining this book's contribution to developing migration scholarship. Overall, this study perceives migrant social relationships as a dynamic complex which includes local and cross-border, 'bonding' and 'bridging' (Ryan 2011) components and does not seek to reduce migrant relationships down to individual elements at the expense of other important factors.

In sum, this book explores post-Soviet Russian-speaking migration to London, which is a novel, valuable, yet underexplored field. It considers the social and spatial connections active in global migration, and seeks to address migrants' informal relationships which are localised in London but have both local and spatially distanciated origins. This book illuminates the construction of social ties and the dynamics which pervade those ties in practice, thereby enriching the understanding of urban sociality within the super-diversity of London. The main ideas of this work stem from acknowledging the complexity of the ways in which contemporary migrants rely upon friendship in their decision making, practices of mobility and daily lives in a particular host society. This complexity cannot be fully grasped by theories of transnationalism, or accounts of ethnic communities. However, it is possible to get closer to understanding migrant social relationships through attending to the variety of close informal relationships in different locations as they exist between different subjects.

Chapter 1
Limits of transnationalism

In the past couple of decades the world has been described by social scientists as being spanned by multiple, intersecting, border-crossing connections between people and places. Social, cultural, and political processes are complex and flexible; identity and belonging are being negotiated through invoking notions of imagined communities, hybridity, flux, and the multiple positioning of subjects. In this respect, migration issues are becoming a much discussed theme in the discourse of globalisation. 'Global cities' are regarded as places with the highest concentration of flows of people, ideas, and capital, and as popular destinations where new migrant populations settle. Such global cities exemplify the condition of 'super-diversity', which manifests an extreme level of diversification between and within various communities along an increasing number of lines (Vertovec 2007b). In this context, contemporary migrants are viewed as highly mobile subjects who maintain enhanced cross-border connections, while ethnic and national diasporic ties can potentially lose some of their cohesive force. This book critically tackles this increasing diversity, the growth of transnationalism, the complex and dynamic social ties sustained and developed by some contemporary migrants, and the proclaimed decline of the ethnic/national 'migrant community'.

Reflecting on the concept of transnationalism, this chapter will add to the critique of the term and its increasingly diffuse application, analysing the limitations of its usage established by many theorists. I will underline the transnational practices that are, to varying extents, characteristic of different social groups and nationalities. Migrants' level of transnational engagement varies, and is dependent on a range of factors such as 'migration channel and legal status, migration and settlement history, community structure and gendered patterns of contact, political circumstances in the homeland, economic means and more' (Vertovec 2007b: 1043). By attending to the diversity of migrants' social networks, I seek to go beyond viewing migrants as practicing homogenous transnational kinship connections. The study of social networks provides a more refined optic with which to conceptualise migration and transnationalism. The premise here is that transnational practices are present to varying degrees, and may even not be necessarily present in most recent migration trends. I also argue for a more nuanced constitution of migrant social connections and their participation in social processes within urban space. One of the key points is that enhanced mobility and daily life in a super-diverse city can promote the re-imagining or re-establishing of a community's national boundedness, where migrants' existing ideas about 'otherness' are influenced by the new environment, the struggle for better life conditions, and the protection of identities threatened by the uncertainties of globalised society. However, moving to a city with a diverse population and participation in its everyday sociality can also involve an acceptance of that diversity and even active participation within its vibrant dynamics. Hence, I suggest focusing on how migrants, as part of the multifaceted population of contemporary London, perceive and build relationships with the city's various inhabitants.

In addition to establishing the theoretical context of transnationalism which this study develops and critiques, this chapter also considers changing patterns in global mobility, with ever increasing numbers of mobile subjects, certain new characteristics attributed to migrants, and the persistence and development of problems in intercultural communication.

London: a super-diverse city

The research that this book is based upon took place among Russian-speaking migrants in London. The characteristics of London that make it such a popular object for migration studies are manifested in its highly stratified population, a constant influx of migrants, and the presence of a variety of different cultures and languages within one city. In this regard, it cannot be compared with any other British city.

The increase in the quantity and diversity of contemporary migration flows to London pose a challenge to traditional notions of ethnicity and/or nationality, which are no longer sufficient to analyse the intricate super-diversity found in the city. 'Super-diversity' is a concept that has been used to describe the complex nature of contemporary London's population. As Vertovec (2007b: 1029) argues, super-diversity is 'a dynamic interplay of variables among an increased number of new, small and scattered, multiple-origin, transnationally connected, socio-economically differentiated and legally stratified immigrants who have arrived over the last decade'. New immigrant groups have appeared on Britain's migrant scene. They differ from previous migrants from Commonwealth countries or former colonial territories in that they are smaller, less organised, highly differentiated and do not have similar historical links with Britain (Vertovec, 2007b: 1029). The term 'super-diverse' has arisen in response to contemporary changes in the UK's immigration profile, in which East European migration is an important factor. Conventional distinctions between 'black and white' can no longer explain adequately the complexity of London's social hierarchies (McDowell 2008a, 2008b). Essentially, the super-diverse UK exhibits a multiplicity of more subtle, less visible degrees of distinction among migrants. Because of changes in the UK population, economy and geopolitical shifts that have taken place since the Second World War, the country has a unique demographic situation, at the epicentre of which is London's extremely diverse population.

One of the key features of super-diversity is that diversity is a characteristic found within ethnic/national groups, and is not merely a state that encompasses a relationship between them. This is in addition to the diversity of migrants themselves, who cannot necessarily be identified purely in terms of their ethnicity or national origin. This situation is related to the British migration regulations which create and reinforce differentiations among migrants by granting access to the labour market and social welfare to some groups, but not to others. As a result, stratified migrant groups may include people who came to the UK via different migration channels, have different legal statuses, take up different positions in labour market hierarchies, are members of different generations, and have different personal migration histories. Super-diversity is also a reflection of migrants' settlement patterns. Vertovec (2007b: 1041) underlines that only a few nationalities are highly concentrated in certain areas of London. Concentrations of ethnic minorities are described as 'local' rather than 'bunched together in particular parts of the city' (Buck et al. 2002: 46). Migrants do not necessarily settle in close proximity to their compatriots in contemporary London.

Another dimension of urban super-diversity's complexity is differentiation in levels of transnational engagement. The increase in transnationalism takes place on different levels: on the one hand, international communication and transactions establish the city's role in the global economy; on the other hand, new networks of international migration establish connections between cities located in different countries (Wills et al. 2010: 28). Although transnationalism has grown in the past years, it is conditioned by a multitude of factors: 'migration channel and legal status (e.g. refugees or undocumented persons may find it harder to maintain certain ties abroad), migration and settlement history, community structure and gendered patterns of contact, political circumstances in the homeland, economic means and more' (Vertovec 2007: 1043). The spatial distribution of migrants' social networks, similarly, can change over time, from more transnational to more localised, and vice versa; the dynamism of these changes varies for different social networks of migrants with different economic and cultural capital (Ryan et al. 2008: 684-686). The presence of many cultures and nationalities in the city space and breaking up the conventional black/white divisions between migrants is a source of new patterns of segregation. New patterns of inequalities and prejudice are the result of complex race and class relationships. Recent and varied inflows of migrants to the UK have brought in new forms of xenophobia, including those among the British towards newcomers, and among previous generation ethnic minorities towards the newest ones. Furthermore, there are emerging patterns of racism among new migrants themselves which are directed against the British and older ethnic minorities. McDowell (2008b: 34) stages 'the current hierarchy of suitability and appropriateness between new A8 white Europeans, older migrants, people of colour and British BME ['black and minority ethnic'] workers' as a new problematic issue for the intergroup community and workplace relations in Britain. Keith (2005a: 177) stresses that London is increasingly witnessing new migrant flows from the former Soviet bloc that might disrupt the conventional binary framing of BME and 'white' communities. As intercultural relationships are becoming more complex with a growing diversity of white migrants arriving in the country, whiteness itself is becoming a problematised and contested category, implicated in a politics of domination, and resulting in 'the establishment of hierarchies of whiteness' (McDowell 2008a, 2008b, 2009). These particular features of London lead to the establishment of a special atmosphere and are connected with the formation of special attitudes towards the city. A place with such a diverse population offers possibilities both for communication and conflict, within and between various communities and groups.

This study analyses how migrants' close personal relationships both function within and are exemplary of this super-diversity, with its many potential benefits and, indeed, its many potential problems. More precisely, I am interested in how the proclaimed decline of the ethnic/national 'migrant community' feeds into the ways in which contemporary migrants rely upon, maintain, develop or contest their close social ties, be they between or within migrant groups in the super-diverse city. Before outlining the status of transnationalism in contemporary migration under the conditions of super-diversity, it is necessary to introduce briefly the population that this research is focused on: Russian-speakers in London and their place within this diversity.

Russian-speaking migrants in London

The numbers of migrants to the UK from post-Soviet countries increased drastically in the years following the break-up of the Soviet Union, particularly since the beginning of the 21st century. The largest national groups are, primarily, from the Baltic states (Lithuania, Latvia and Estonia): migration to the UK from these countries rose following the 2004 EU accession,[1] which eventually allowed citizens of A8 countries free movement and the gradual lifting of restrictions on access to work, housing rights and social benefits. A significant number of Russian and Ukrainian migrants have also arrived, as have smaller populations from Kazakhstan, Azerbaijan and Belarus.

A large share of the UK's current post-Soviet population is Russian-speaking. This includes both people who consider Russian as their main language and those who are bilingual/multilingual and have a command of Russian.

Finding reliable data from the period up to 2010 concerning the size of this population of Russian-speakers is difficult. In 2007, a mapping exercise by the International Organisation for Migration (IOM)

---

1   In 2004, eight Central and Eastern European countries (the Czech Republic, Estonia, Hungary, Latvia, Lithuania, Poland, Slovakia, and Slovenia), and two Mediterranean countries (Malta and Cyprus) joined the European Union, which was followed by increased labour migration from some of these countries to Western Europe. Romania and Bulgaria joined in 2007.

calculated that the UK's population included 300,000 Russians. This widely quoted estimate is highly speculative and was drawn from sources like visa statistics, the Russian embassy and 'unofficial assessment'. Moreover, the report itself is contradictory. The report's claim that there are 300,000 Russians living in the UK is undermined by some figures quoted on the following page. These figures claim that there are 300,000 Russians in London, as well as an estimated 40,000 in Manchester, 35,000 in Scotland, and 13,000 each in Birmingham, Cambridge, Bristol and Brighton—which brings us to over 400,000 overall. These numbers provoked scepticism. Given that the 2011 Census revealed that there were 579,000 Polish-born people in Britain, it is hard to imagine the Russian population being anywhere near a similar level.

The Office for National Statistics' (ONS) estimates and data from the 2011 Census have significantly clarified the situation about the size of post-Soviet, Russian and Russian-speaking populations. While the data is still imprecise, it provides a general picture of the state of this migrant population.

It is worth presenting some statistical data here. Table 1.1 is based on estimates of the post-Soviet population resident in the UK since 2012 (ONS 2013b).

Table 1.1 Post-Soviet population resident in the UK from 2012, thousands (ONS 2013b)

Country	Estimate by nationality	Estimate by country of birth
Armenia	3	2
Azerbaijan	2	1
Belarus	6	2
Estonia	9	7
Georgia	1	1
Kazakhstan	5	4
Kyrgyzstan	1	-
Latvia	69	70
Lithuania	130	140
Moldova	3	2
Mongolia	1	1
Russia	46	36
Ukraine	22	12
Uzbekistan	3	2

A more nuanced examination of the quantity and distribution of Russian-speakers must account for the significant issue of a subject's self-identification as a Russian-speaker, considering that such self-identification has both pragmatic and political value. Table 1.2 is based upon 2011 Census data by the ONS and provides data on main language (i.e. first or preferred) use in England and Wales.

Table 1.2 Main language, 2011 Census (ONS 2013a).

Language	Numbers (England and Wales)	% of users	Numbers (London)	% of users
Russian	67,366	0.1	26,603	0.3
Ukrainian	6,578	0.0	2,912	0.0
Lithuanian	85,469	0.2	35,341	0.5
Latvian	31,523	0.1	4,452	0.1
Estonian	3,398	-	1,192	-

These numbers are enough to demonstrate that the population that identifies itself as Russian-speaking is quite small; not all migrants from the post-Soviet state who have a command of Russian would consider themselves Russophone (i.e. speakers of Russian either natively or by preference).

The geographical distribution of the relative percentages of Russian-speakers in various areas is shown on an interactive map based on Census results (Rogers 2013). In the UK, for example, the highest concentrations of Russian-speakers, according to this map and statistical data, are in London, King's Lynn and West Norfolk, Oxford, Harrogate, Boston, Kingston upon Hull. In London, high concentrations of Russian-speakers in 2011 were in Westminster, Kensington and Chelsea, Tower Hamlets, Newham, Wandsworth, Southwark and Barnet. Another interactive map visualised the top 10 London language communities on Twitter, including Russian, in the summer of 2012 (see Cheshire 2012). It demonstrates, for example, concentrations of Russian-speaking Tweets in central London (some of these could be tourists, though, as it was the summer of the Olympics).

Statistical data and maps are still not completely reliable sources of information concerning post-Soviet or Russian-speaking migration to the UK. The data may be incomplete and imprecise for a number of reasons: the small size of the groups studied, gaps in methodology (for example, the Labour Force Survey which is one of the ONS's data sources does not include students in halls of residence), lack or difficulty of access to particular groups (for example, irregular migrants). Nevertheless, they are helpful for creating a general picture of this population. The Russian-speaking population is quite small, even considering that the data underestimates the real numbers and only includes people who identify themselves as Russian-speakers. The majority of this population lives in London, followed by the South East and East of the country. It is likely that the majority of this population is not only Russophone but Russian by origin and/or (to a lesser extent) nationality.

But why focus on Russian-speakers in this present study? Indeed, it might have seemed easier to concentrate on, say, Russian nationals. However, it is Russian-speakers which are a significant part of London's super-diversity as a highly diverse population with a multitude of internal divisions and groupings. The above-noted data implies that it would be incorrect to speak about a unified community of post-Soviet migrants or a coherent community of Russian-speakers in the UK. One cannot speak about the existence of a Russian diaspora as such, provided that 'diaspora' is understood as a group meeting the following criteria: (1) dispersion in space; (2) orientation to a 'homeland' as an authoritative source of value, identity, and loyalty; and (3), the preservation of a distinct identity within the host society (Brubaker 2005: 5-6). In the case of Russian-speakers from post-Soviet countries currently living in the UK, one can use the term 'community' only as a heuristic device rather than a definition of a concrete, unified, tightly knit and homogenous group. 'Community' denotes the commonalities of historical, linguistic, sociocultural, ethnic, and national character that exist among most of the recent Russian-speaking migrants to the UK, but does not automatically imply that these commonalities are seen as necessary prerequisites for the formation of social networks in practice. This nuanced use of 'community' can be explained by the internal differences and tensions among members of this loosely defined group which do not allow to approach it as a unified entity. Since the mid-2000s, researchers and journalists (Byford 2009a, 2009b; Grechaninova 2007; Kopnina 2005; Morgunova 2009) have started using the term 'Russian-speakers' while referring to this network of post-Soviet migrants. It may mark the historical commonalities of their backgrounds, including the 'imagined Soviet Union' as the key reference point, similarities of sociocultural experiences, as well as the role of the Russian language still being a *lingua franca* for many contemporary migrants from different countries. However, this term is also a contested one: while it is used unproblematically by most Russians in their identifications of self and others, for the members of the rest of the post-Soviet population Russophony is a controversial phenomenon that makes self-identification as 'Russian-speakers' less relevant to bi- and multilingual people's experience and perceptions of self.

It is also worth mentioning that Russians in particular are often described as tending to socialise within small informal networks rather than aiming to participate in large, more formal groups that are organised 'from above'. In this regard, the very idea of belonging to a 'community' is rejected by many post-Soviet migrants, and not merely those migrants who can be legitimately identified as Russian. Class divisions, gender, generational differences, national identities and political positions (especially most recently in light of the Russia-Ukraine conflict that is ongoing at the time of the writing) all contribute to the fragmentation of this population.

These London-based migrants are characterised by the presence of people from all social strata and occupational categories, a dispersed character of settlement, and sociality patterns that stem from the stratified nature of this migrant group and result in it being a loose collection of 'subcommunities' (Kopnina 2005). Byford (2009a: 55) argues that the 'diasporisation' of post-Soviet Russian migrants in Britain is not based directly on a Russian *ethnos*, state, national culture, or even language; but rather united by 'a historically-specific socio-cultural background shared by the generation of people born in the former USSR [...], whose formative identifications are therefore rooted, somewhat peculiarly, in a state and society that are no more, and whose lifeworlds span the distinctive juncture between late socialism and postsocialism'). He describes the UK's Russian-speaking migrant population as characterised by a high degree of social stratification, the differing extents to which migrants rely upon their community and the fluidity of boundaries

(Byford 2009a). Such characteristics imply that this population is relatively open to representatives and institutions not of post-Soviet origin. Moreover, the Russian-speaking population is geographically scattered around London, settling according to social class rather than proximity to compatriots. Russian nationals, in particular, are described as people 'obsessed with secrecy and discretion at all levels of the society': they may engage in networking with compatriots at cultural events or in professional associations and clubs, but always maintain a certain degree of privacy (Dmitrieva and Yuferova 2011).

Middle-class Russian-speakers form a significant part of London's Former Soviet Union (FSU) population. Their migrant life is often the result of a desire for more comfortable surroundings, the opportunities provided by London's highly rated educational institutions and the city's employment prospects, and is less likely to be motivated by financial needs or political pressures in their home country. However, they are part of what Kopnina describes as an 'invisible community'. This invisibility stems from a number of factors: the lack of academic research on contemporary migration by Russian-speakers; their small number in comparison with other migrant and diasporic groups; the relatively recent formation of this population (late 1990s-early 2000s); their white European complexion; and their socially stratified character, where smaller social groups live their own lives and rarely engage in close interaction with compatriots. Other parts of this population, such as oligarchs and the super-rich, political refugees, activists, and irregular migrants are usually more 'visible' in the media and academic research. However, middle-class professionals from the former Soviet Union are paid much less attention: indeed, they are comparably 'unproblematic', much less vocal about their activities and their impact, and form a small part of the general inflow of professional migrants. But they are the new and mobile East European migrants who engage in transnational networks and add some qualitative difference to London's social, ethnic and linguistic tapestry. Coming back to the question of the relationship between the proclaimed decline of the ethnic/national 'migrant community', the growth of transnationalism, and the complex relationships that people develop, maintain, and rely upon in the super-diverse city, this study now turns to the concept of transnationalism and its limitations.

Transnationalism: introducing a popular concept in migration studies

Transnationalism studies began in the early 1990s as a critique of classical migration theories that had assumed a linear progression of movement and change. Migrants were regarded as individuals who left one community in order to settle in another; and were understood as belonging to only one set of social relations at a time. In contrast to these theories, the concept of transnationalism arose from research that addressed migrants' ties to their home *and* receiving country. Given the multiple attachments and diverse social relations experienced by migrants towards their societies of origin and settlement, researchers of transnationalism rejected the traditional paradigm, claiming that sending and receiving societies should be understood as constituting a single field of analysis (Ho 2008: 1287). Glick Schiller, an early pioneer of research in this field, defined transnationalism as 'the processes by which immigrants forge and sustain multi-stranded social relations that link together their societies of origin and settlement' (Glick Schiller *et al.* 1995: 484). The migrants active within these processes were accordingly designated *trans*migrants, whom Glick Schiller defined as migrants 'whose daily lives depend on a multiple and constant interconnections across national borders and whose public identities are configured in relationship to more than one nation-state' (1995: 48). Such multi-stranded, border spanning social relations between origin and settlement societies encompass a broad spectrum of socio-economic phenomena. Guarnizo (1997: 288) suggested that the transnational optic encompasses 'a series of economic, sociocultural and political practical and discursive relations that transcend the territorially bound jurisdiction of the nation-state'; and Portes *et al.* (1999: 219) regarded the term as entailing the economic, political, and sociocultural occupations and activities that require regular, long-term contacts across borders.

Conceptualising contemporary migrant communities as transnational has become a well-established practice for social scientists. The increase of transnationalism is now seen in parallel with globalisation itself, the growth of global cities as key points of capital accumulation, communication and control, as well as the development of technology and communication (Glick Schiller *et al.* 1995; Vertovec 2007a, 2007b). Such calibrations of the breadth of the transnational panoply have been accompanied by research into particular tendencies active within its complex matrix. Guarnizo and Smith (1998) juxtaposed 'transnationalism from below', or the everyday, grounded practices of individuals and groups, with 'transnationalism from above', or global governance and economic activities. Bauböck (2003) and Van Bochove (2012) have focused on political transnationalism, exploring migrants' involvement in home country politics through electoral participation, lobbying, protest rallies, consumer boycotts and overlapping political memberships. Vertovec has also stressed the significance of the political in transnationalism, arguing that the transnational amounts to a global public space of political engagement in addition to a means of (re)constructing 'place' or locality (Vertovec 1999). It has also been argued that transnational connectivity implies border-spanning links and interactions between people and institutions that include sustaining ties with local communities and families 'back home' through travel, communication and the exchange of material resources (Levitt

2001); whilst Sklair (2000) has stressed the importance of transnational corporations, for which transnationalism is effectively an avenue for the exchange and flow of capital. Portes *et al.* (1999) and Vertovec (2007a, 2007b) have foregrounded the normative dimension of transnationalism, whereby the many acts and means of keeping in touch with relatives and communities of origin has become a norm for many contemporary migrants. In addition to such accounts of transnationalism and its border spanning social formations, it has been suggested that the term designates a type of consciousness that involves subjects' multiple identifications; and amounts to a mode of cultural reproduction where the focus is on the constructed, contested and fluid nature of cultures (Hall 1990). Despite the immense range of critical uses of transnationalism, it is important to differentiate the term from certain totalising accounts of globalisation. Researchers of transnationalism have, at times, provided sweeping theoretical statements and avoided analytical focus on the empirical phenomena of local communities themselves. With such a broad range of approaches to transnationalism, the scale of these studies has been a topic for discussion for some researchers, and quite a few argue that more attention should be paid to empirical research of small-scale movements and groups. Favell (2001: 397) suggests providing systematic empirical evidence for studies of globalisation in order to get rid of 'fruitless social theoretical speculations' common to globalisation theorists, and thus to focus on migration and transnational networks as 'very real' phenomena. It has been noted that almost any contemporary book about globalisation is a mild exercise in megalomania (Appadurai 1996: 18). Smith (2001) underlines that theorists of 'global cities' such as Saskia Sassen or David Harvey present incomplete social constructions of globalisation. Such theoretical constructions privilege the functional logics of global capital 'from above' and fail to address local and transnational practices 'from below'. Smith has argued that local communities are dynamic, and rejects those critics who understand the local as distinct from transnational flows of ideas, information, financial transactions, and religious and cultural movements (Smith 2001). Portes (2000: 254) stresses that transnational processes are created by common people as a response to globalisation, and their economic activities are fuelled by and inseparable from capitalist expansion: consumption standards, popular culture, the labour needs of the developed world, and the proliferation of its productive investment. Marginalizing or excluding everyday cultural practices tends to deny their importance as historical models of urban agency.

This is study consistent with such demands that the transnational critic should address the everyday transnationalism of its subjects, and engages with the concept of the transnational 'from below' rather than 'from above'. The following analysis focuses on individuals and small-scale social networks; and the role of both local and cross-border connections and interactions in their lives. In the next section, the focus is on those people and social groups that are often taken as objects of transnational studies, and the limitations of conventional approaches to transmigrants.

Who is a transmigrant?

Transnationalism studies include not only research on global corporations and the 'transnational capitalist class' (Sklair 2000, 2002), but also case studies of migrant groups and their lives in the contexts of border-crossing activities, transnational communities and world cities. Glick Schiller *et al.* (1995: 50) justify studying migration 'rather than abstract cultural flows or representations', and focus on individuals' and families' life experiences. Portes (2000: 254) underlines the significance of transnationalism studies as a tool for research not only of world system structures, but also for the analysis of everyday networks and patterns of social relationships that emerge in and around those structures. Favell also suggests stepping aside from macro-level data to study how 'real individuals, with everyday family lives and human relationships, could actually live out the lives predicted for them by the macro economic data about flows and networks' (Favell 2003: 11). Glick Schiller and Çaglar (2009: 180) suggest focusing on individual migrants, the networks they form, and the social fields created by these networks, which they understand as systems of social relations rather than spatial metaphors. Following these theorists, the focus here is on people as social actors that produce culture, participate in micro-networks of social action and attend to social processes taking place in contemporary cities on a small-scale level.

The unit of analysis for transnational studies is an individual or a group of people who regularly engage in cross-border activities (Glick Schiller et al. 1995; Guarnizo 1997; Levitt 2001; Portes et al. 1999). Smith (2001) regards transnational migrants as participating in communicative actions connecting localities beyond borders, engaging in transnational practices, and establishing translocal relations within historically and geographically specific points of origin and destination. 'Intimate circles and small networks can be involved here; the transnational is not always immense in scale' (Hannerz 1996: 89). The transnational character of movements does not mean the attenuation and eventual loss of links to a migrant's place of origin. The new features of contemporary migration include the increasing back-and-forth global movements of people in a huge variety of forms and frequencies. A new image of migrants appears—an image of those who search for work for a better life, who are not driven by displacement, who might regularly return back to where they came from not because they failed but because they planned it; and who are therefore 'postponing an answer to the question where they really belong, or simply making the question irrelevant' (Hannerz 1992: 246). At the same time, being transnational does not mean being unable to assimilate in the host society. Engagement in cross-border activities can be combined with being a well-integrated, naturalised, and economically successful resident of a host country (Portes et al. 2002: 294; Vertovec 2007b: 1046). In this respect, transnationalism implies enhanced connectivity with multiple locations, ideally not at the expense of ghettoisation or becoming cut off from some connections. Indeed, simultaneous involvement in communities across borders is one of the elements of transnationalism.

Initially, transnationalism studies have mainly focused (and still often do) on Third World nationals (Latin American, Caribbean and Filipino migrants), with particular attention given to kinship networks and connections (Glick Schiller et al. 1995; Gruner-Domic 2011; Levitt 2001; Portes 2000; Soehl and Waldinger 2010). These migrants were, according to Favell (2003: 14), new heroes of 'globalisation from below', and the main focus of these studies was on economic and cultural networks, business transactions and remittances, as well as political and social influence on events back home. Other studies address elite groups in the financial, media and service industries (Favell 2003: 16; Sklair 2002). The role of education abroad for the formation of transnational professionals has been underlined, often intrinsically concentrating on rather elite groups pursuing education abroad (Hall 2011; Waters 2007). Entrepreneurs and their transnationalism, as a form of contemporary economic adaptation based on the mobilisation of their cross-country social networks, shape another strand of research (Portes et al. 2002).

Many transnationalism scholars focused on the new migrant underclasses and the emergent 'global elites', as they are viewed as the social groups whose mobility is most noticeably motivated by the employment requirements of world cities in the developed West. Far less academic interest has been directed at those subjects who live between these extremes. Indeed, transnationalism may be characteristic of a larger variety of migrants than these two groups. Recently, attention has focused upon a more 'middling' kind of transnationalism, examining those who live between the polar opposites of marginalised Third World migrants and global elites: specifically, middle-class professionals. 'Middling' migrants belong to the middle class both in home and host countries, and are drawn to world cities not only because of labour market attractions, but also due to the cities' cultural and social features (Blunt 2007; Conradson and Latham 2005a, 2005b). These are the people for whom potential economic benefits are not the only or the primary consideration. So-called 'aesthetic' motivations play a significant role which has led some researchers to call them 'lifestyle migrants' (Knowles and Harper 2009). Whereas some studies of the transmigration of society's highest and lowest strata have analysed institutional questions, research of 'middling' transmigration has emphasised the geographies of individuals' everyday lives (Waters 2007), as well as the dynamics of global cities and the peculiarities of transnational migrants' everyday lives (Blunt 2007; Smith 2001, 2005). Conradson and Latham (2005a, 2005b) have emphasised the importance of studying networks, connections and relationships as evolving everyday practices of middle-class transnationalism. World cities are more and more frequently approached as hosts to diverse middle-class migrant populations and, although such mobility is still practiced by a limited number of people, it has become a 'normal' middle-class activity (Scott 2006: 1107). Scott also underlines the much more 'complex and messy' character of middle-class transnational migration, particularly with regard to previous studies of corporate managers and cleaners. Therefore, I do not claim here that all middle-class migrants tend to be transnational; rather, I suggest that the extent to which these people may rely upon, sustain and develop their cross-border connections needs detailed attention.

'Ordinary' people—those who do not represent the extreme ends of social hierarchies either in home countries or in the receiving society, and who are middle class both 'here' and 'there', mostly educated, and 'drawn to the city as much by what it offers them in lifestyle and personal experience terms as by any narrow economic calculus' (Conradson and Latham 2005a: 290)—constitute a large part of contemporary migration and need more attention from migration and transnationalism theorists. However, before this analysis proceeds to address this need for an empirically grounded inquiry into the lives of 'middling' transmigrants, there are certain limitations of the concept of transnationalism that need to be attended to.

Critique of transnationalism

The main critique of transnationalism studies has warned, primarily, that the pervasiveness of the concept 'may make it appear as if everybody is "going transnational", which is far from being the case' (Levitt 2001; Portes 2000: 264; Scott 2006; Vertovec 1999, 2001). Concentrating too much on transnational subjects may give the false impression that transnationalism is the main way of the political and economic adaptation of migrants. Portes argues against simply re-labelling contemporary migration as transnational. He explains the proliferation of the use of this term by the largely anthropological origin of the research on it, which has provided a large number of case studies of specific immigrant groups, creating 'rich descriptions but obscuring the scope' of the phenomenon (Portes 2001: 182). The novelty of transnationalism as a phenomenon has also been questioned. This research field's problems stem from failing to notice that transnational migrants are only part of migrant communities in general, their cross-border practices are similar to those from the past, and the label of transnational is used for multiple sets of different activities (Portes 2001; Portes *et al.* 1999). On the one hand, contemporary migration is usually characterised by larger numbers of people migrating and ease of communication. Yet on the other hand, only some migrants engage in cross-border activities regularly, and take part in the economic, political and cultural lives of their host and home countries to such an extent that allows them to be designated as transnational. As mentioned in the above discussion of super-diversity, the level of transnational engagement may vary among different individuals and communities (Vertovec 1999, 2007b). Smith (2005: 88) also underlines the heterogeneity of transmigration even within the same migrating 'nationality' and within the same transnational city. In addition, not all migrants who maintain regular ties across borders belong to the ideal type of transmigrant; that is, a figure who maintains a balance of enhanced connectivity with several places without the risk of being segregated from any of these communities. Transnational links may weaken or disappear over time, as some empirical research shows (Ryan *et al.* 2008: 684-685): the dynamism of migrants' social networks and the shifting balance between local/transnational connections has yet to be fully researched.

Claims that 'cheap transport and advances in telecommunications have allowed migrants to maintain, as never before, extensive social, economic and political ties with places of origin or fellow members of global diasporas' (Vertovec 2007a: 7), or that migrants' entry to host countries is now less restrictive (Levitt 2001) seem to be only relatively applicable, considering global inequalities that are often reinforced by immigration regimes. Ong (1999: 134) mentions that boundaries are less flexible for 'less well-heeled individuals': there are structural limits and personal costs to flexible citizenship. McDowell (2008b: 495) underlines that labour is not as free to move as capital, given that it is differentiated by age, skills, skin colour and gender. The particular case of Britain proves that migrants face different structural limits of access to transnationalism. The British labour market is relatively open to European Union nationals, yet other nationals face greater restrictions, thus reinforcing inequalities in power and access to resources (McDowell 2009; Wills *et al.*

2010). Their different positions are conditioned by both institutional structures and their everyday practices. In other words, transnational studies may be criticised for generalising the ease of individuals' communication and travel. While there are more opportunities for mobility and cross-border activity now, these opportunities are not universally available. Continuing and developing this critique, this study underlines that the phenomenon of transnationalism is dependent upon a variety of structural factors and personal motivations, and therefore has to be approached carefully.

Considering the complexity of transnationalism, Vertovec (2001: 576) suggests that rather than having a single theory, it would make sense to theorise a typology of transnationalisms and the conditions that affect them. Attempts to distinguish transnational practices from non-transnational and to make a taxonomy of its degrees of variation have taken place (Dahinden 2009; Morawska 2004; Scott 2006; Soehl and Waldinger 2010; Van Bochove et al. 2010). These studies detail the balance between transnational and assimilation strategies, link social morphologies to the social positioning of migrants, and eventually claim that contemporary migration has achieved an increasingly diverse 'human face' (Scott 2006: 1108), and can no longer fit into the traditional paradigm of economically motivated migration. Researchers agree that migrants vary in the intensity of their cross-border connections, and emphasise that the majority maintain only some degree of transnationalism. The reasons for this state of affairs are numerous, and include the location of key social ties, cultural practices, citizenship status, and the costs associated with different types of cross-border activity (Soehl and Waldinger 2010).

The arguments debating the novelty and universality of transnationalism are closely connected with another important idea for this book. The emergence of transnationalism has been put into context of the global restructuring of capital, the growth of world cities, and the 'diminished significance of national boundaries in the production and distribution of objects, ideas, and people' (Glick Schiller *et al.* 1995). Soysal (1994) derives from transnational discourse a model of postnational citizenship, where personhood and human rights act 'as a world-level organizing principle' that governs the incorporation of contemporary migrants. For Soysal, this organising principle is of far greater significance than national rights. That is not to say, however, that she conceptualises the transnational community as a tightly bounded group rooted in a vague ethnic or cultural solidarity that lacks local connections or identities (Soysal 1994: 339). Similarly, Vertovec (2001: 580) argues that transnationalism offers a possibility of unfixing nation-derived identities and 'arriving at new, cosmopolitan perspectives on culture and belonging'.

However, as a critique of these claims, the 'age of transnationalism' is increasingly considered by some researchers as a time when nation-states are relevant and influential in migration contexts (Glick Schiller et al. 1995: 59; Koopmans 2004). Theorists have been criticised for suggesting that that the role of the nation-state has radically changed with the advent of globalisation, and that migration has become more influenced by supranational institutions and transnational discourses (Sassen 2001; Soysal 1994). Researchers note that at the same time contemporary transnational cultural processes and movements have been accompanied by an increase in identity politics. Favell's study (2008) on professionals' free movement in Europe noted that, despite the denationalised 'European' identity and cosmopolitan self that can result from free movement across borders, so-called 'Eurostars' eventually find themselves immersed into renationalising processes. Lifestyles imposed by nation-states, 'the basic everyday durability of nationally specific practices and identities in organizing the behaviour of people' (Favell 2003: 11), are reluctant to change, despite the proclaimed trends of the free movement of people, information, and capital in globalising Europe. Globalising processes go together with the 'pre-eminence of exclusive, bounded, essentialised nationalisms' (Appadurai 1993 cited in Glick Schiller et al. 1995: 52). The reconstruction and reinvention of national identities take place as a part of what Anderson termed long-distance nationalism (1992), a process that can be supported by border-crossing identities and connections, and the increased possibilities of maintaining these connections. Anderson notes that migrants' 'emotional life and political psychology often remains nostalgically orientated towards a heimat which, thanks to capitalism and late-century technologies, retains a powerful daily grip over them' (1992: 9). The development of transnationalism can intensify this grip: the features of the globalised world are regarded as having made it 'easier than ever before for people of common origins to maintain ties and identities even as they moved', which makes nation, ethnicity and race powerful forces in contemporary societies (Cornell and Hartmann 2007: 4). In fact, mobility can contribute to reinforcing all kinds of xenophobic and oppressive beliefs, instead of, or in addition to, developing openness and cosmopolitan sociabilites.

When Wimmer and Glick Schiller (2003: 598) argue against methodological nationalism as the naturalisation of the global regime of nation-states by the social sciences, they also warn against 'methodological fluidism', which privileges 'a spiralling rhetorics of deterritorialisation and delocalisation' and neglects concrete geographical locations and socially bounded environments (Wimmer and Glick Schiller (2002: 326). One of the gaps in the first wave of transnational studies was a contrast between the contemporary globalised world and the past. The latter was implicitly assumed to consist of bounded, 'ethnic', homogeneous, and static groups and societies. Urry (2000), for one, has been heavily criticised (Eriksen 2002: 29; Favell 2001; Wimmer and Glick Schiller 2003) for depicting the transnational lifestyle as the prototype for the life of contemporary migrants, in contrast to the supposedly unitary solidity and boundedness of 'societies' of the past. Urry's critics argue that nation-states are still important, even if social life is not necessarily regulated by their boundaries (Levitt and Glick Schiller 2004). Wimmer and Glick Schiller also warn against overestimating the internal homogeneity and boundedness of transnational communities, and overlooking the importance of cross-community interactions as well as the internal divisions of class, gender, region, and politics. Social ties and networks not based upon shared ethnic, national, or ethno-religious identities have been paid considerably less attention.[2] Such limited conceptualisations of migrant groups 'tend to reify and essentialise these communities' (Eriksen 2002: 145; Fenton 2010; Glick Schiller et al. 2011: 598; Wimmer and Glick Schiller 2003: 406). Indeed, privileging diasporic attachments can lead to underreporting those practices, relationships, and identifications that transcend the boundaries of the national or the ethnic. Similarly, assuming that migrants' transnational social fields and networks can be approached as communities can also be a reason for identifying a community as transnational when it is not, or that transnationalism is not significant for the migrants in question. Eriksen (2002: 155) also notes that 'the symbolic reconstruction of a distant homeland is not an inevitable outcome of migration'.

While political claims and practices based upon long-distance nationalism are not uncommon for diasporic actors (Anderson 1992; Glick Schiller and Fouron 1999; Vertovec 1999), it is nonetheless important to acknowledge that such claims and practices are supported by globalisation (Conversi 2012). Ethnic identities and boundaries are not necessarily effaced by globalisation, and can come to the fore in its many processes. Beck (2002: 38) outlines the ethnic globalisation paradox: 'At a time when the world is growing closer together and becoming more cosmopolitan, in which, therefore, the borders and barriers between nations and ethnic groups are being lifted, ethnic identities and divisions are becoming

---

[2] But see Datta 2009; Morosanu 2013b.

stronger once again'. Elsewhere (Beck 2006: 4) he also writes about the emergence of 'introverted forms of nationalism which oppose the 'invasion' of the global world by turning inwards' and promote aggressive intolerance of others. Although they do not aim at military and ideological conquests beyond their borders, these forms usually involve conscious resistance to the cosmopolitanisation of people's life-worlds, to globalisation and globalisers who are perceived as threatening the local form of life of the 'natives'. 'Those involved seek refuge in a strategic 'as-if' essentialism of ethnicity in an attempt to fix the blurred and shifting boundaries between internal and external, us and them' (Beck 2006: 4).

The dense social space of the global city in particular offers possibilities to question the role of transnationalism in respect to identities, social ties and group formation. Amin (2002: 11) warns that hybridisation and facing diversity on an everyday basis do not guarantee the development of intercultural understanding. Keith has noted that 'in the allure of the contemporary global city, cosmopolitanism, diversity and difference shimmer for a moment. Racism, nationalism, ethnic cleansing and xenophobia return as urban nightmares' (2005a: 14). Racialisation can take place in a contemporary city in times of uncertainty, hybridity of ethnic groups, cultures, and localised identities in particular locations, differentiations within the international labour market, and segregating labour policies. In describing the city, Keith uses the metaphors of a theatre where different cultural values, economic and political ideologies, and dynamics of social change are brought together (Keith 2005a: 50); and a competitive arena where mutable ethnic cultures, a concentration of hybridisation and demographic difference all clash with one another (Keith 2005b: 255). The city can be a paradoxical space displaying both intense forms of intolerance and cultural dialogue. The subtle forms of racialisation in London are influenced by a variety of factors, such as the large quantity of migrants, significant differences between income and occupational structure, and complex patterns of social differentiations. Socioeconomic deprivation and the sense of desperation it produces can be triggers for the development of ethnic resentment (Amin 2002: 5). This is particularly true for London with its unequal social structure and high levels of competition in the labour market, both between migrant and non-migrant Londoners.

This makes the focus of this book particularly topical, given the emergence of new East European migration to the UK which has prompted researchers' interest in new patterns of intercultural relationships, transnational connections, and racialisation and cosmopolitan sociabilities. Most of the researchers, however, have concentrated on migrants from post-accession East European countries.[3] Issues of power, social and cultural capital, and 'living with diversity' are central for this body of research. Of the range of migrants from post-accession countries, considerably less has been written about migrants from the Baltic states; and even less on non-EU post-Soviet migrants during the 21st century. [4] While being less

---

[3] UK migration scholarship has paid significant attention to the new East European migration. Wills et al. (2010: 108) write about post-accession East European workers articulating superiority over non-European colleagues 'on the basis of a "European" identity constructed around an extended European Union, and underpinned by issues of race', and whose attitudes combine the racist discourse of home countries and their response to their position in the London labour market. McDowell (2008b: 501) describes problems emerging with the accession of new EU member-states and increased migration from these countries to London: new Europeans interviewed 'were not always tolerant of ethnic Others, leading to intra-class conflict based on ethnicity and skin colour'. Datta and Brickell (2009) explore how Polish builders construct themselves relationally to English builders as they negotiate their place within the labour hierarchies of the building site, and in the London labour market, marking themselves as 'superior' to the English through the versatility of their embodied skills, work ethic, artistic qualities, and finesse in their social interactions. In another paper, Datta (2009) looks at how these builders develop varying cosmopolitanisms in everyday places that are shaped by migrants' transnational histories, nationalistic sentiments, and access to social and cultural capital in specific localised contexts. Social networks and social capital have been major themes (Ryan et a l. 2008; Ryan 2011), as well as the complications thereof (Morosanu 2013a, 2013b).

[4] However, see Byford 2009a, 2009b; Malyutina 2012, 2014; Morgunova 2012. Research on Russian-speaking migrants can often successfully draw inspiration from studies of post-accession East European migrants. These strands of

numerous, however, the recent Russian-speaking migrants from former Soviet states who are studied in this present work are a diverse population, and have been brought together by a multitude of ties and divided by numerous boundaries. This study addresses this apparent lacuna in current migration scholarship and examines the ways in which these people exist within the super-diverse city as social beings, and how cross-border connectivity contributes to their lives.

When seeking to understand how migrant communities function, it is helpful to study the informal social relationships that unfold both within a migrant community and transcend its borders. According to Brubaker (2004: 11), this requires attending to 'groupness as a contextually fluctuating conceptual variable', and not taking 'groups' for granted as idealised collective actors. After authors such as Conradson and Latham (2005a, 2005b), Ryan et al. (2008) and Vertovec (2001), this study demands detailed research of migrants' social relationships in order to understand the 'dynamism, diversity and spatial dispersion of migrants' social networks' (Ryan et al. 2008: 685). In addition, this study recognises the need to highlight connections and disconnections as part of any relationships (be they local or border-crossing) in order to avoid the risk of reifying a given community.

The complexities of contemporary migration and its increasing diversity point to the need to study these constructions of difference that are 'produced and maintained through practices that operate at and across different spatial scales including ideological assumptions, multiple regulatory systems, structures of power and domination and spoken and enacted everyday practices in multiple sites, that operate at both conscious and unconscious levels and open to contestation and negotiation' (McDowell 2008b: 496). At the same

---

research are often faced with similar challenges that are common for these new patterns of UK migration: for example, negotiating whiteness, social capital and social networks, gender and migration.

time, social relations and social networks, small-scale personal interactions and intimacies, companionships and friendships all form an area that can be addressed by social scientists in order to understand their role in transnational processes.

A study of migrant social networks would be incomplete if these social networks were not contextualised amongst the varied dynamics of social interactions and groupings that occur in a multicultural, multi-ethnic, and super-diverse social space like London.

Conclusions

This chapter outlines how the concept of transnationalism has been deployed in descriptions of contemporary migrants' practices, and underlines that the increasing diversity of contemporary migration should be taken into account when critics seek to analyse cross-border activity and the formation of transnational communities. I argue here that the concept of transnationalism has to be approached with greater attention to the particular circumstances of migration, and must consider the stratified and heterogeneous character of contemporary migrant communities. While the diversity of migrants is great, research is still often confined to certain social groups, usually either disadvantaged or quite affluent. More attention is needed to 'middling transnationalism', that is, the 'ordinary people' who constitute a growing share of today's migration.

The key point of this chapter is that the advances of globalisation do not bring universal change to all kinds of potential migrants, but rather add to the diversification of migration in terms of the inequalities which result from structural factors and personal motivations affecting mobility, maintaining of ethnic and national identities, and the (re-)emergence of boundaries. Different migratory situations may challenge and resist the development of postnational (Soysal 1994) or denationalised (Favell 2008) identities and practices, and increased cross-border connectivity can support this state of affairs.

It has also been emphasised that the transnational element of migrant sociality should not be overestimated. Taking into account the assumption that with the development of contemporary migration studies the notion of transnationalism is becoming diffuse and loosely interpreted, this chapter has suggested a more nuanced approach to contemporary migration. The aim here is to show a wider picture of migrants' practices of sociality, where the actual variety of relationships among compatriots can be quite diverse and not universally transnational.

In order to meet these demands, there is a need to pay special attention to the development and proliferation of migrants' personal networks, and consider the dynamics of their relationships with both compatriots and 'others' ; that is, the non-migrant local population and other migrants. Detailed research of migrants' social networks is necessary if we are to understand contemporary mobility trends. A balanced analysis that takes into account all aspects of migrant sociality will eventually show the conditions and limitations of the development of transnationalism, as well as its possible risks and benefits.

The next chapter discusses the role of ethnicity in migrant social connections, and will continue to develop possible conceptualisations of relationships that might be based upon something more nuanced than mutual ethnic or national affiliation, or even migrant status. It will serve to connect the conceptual questions of migrants' social networks in terms of their boundaries, functioning, cohesion and divisiveness, and spatial and social positioning. These factors are discussed in terms of the variety of ways in which migrants' relationships with compatriots and non-migrant/non-compatriot Londoners are imagined, constructed, and reconstructed.

Chapter 2
Ethnicity and social relationships

In the previous chapter, I have emphasised that seeing migrant populations as communities—more precisely, as social groups that are bounded by internal solidarity, and tend to occupy a certain social niche—leads to reification and essentialisation of migrant sociality. There can be too many divisions and differences among the members of assumed communities; there can be a multitude of important social connections between migrants and non-migrants; and there can be few significant social connections between migrants. In addition, it is wrong to suppose that globalisation offers equal opportunities of mobility, employment, and communication to people differentiated by education, class, and citizenship.

This has resulted in superficial conclusions concerning the nature and significance of people's cross-border connections and the balance between transnational and local ties. The risk is not only overlooking the importance of spatial factors such as distance and proximity in relationships, but also neglecting the importance of other kinds of relationships and identifications. Considering this, this study pays more attention to ethnicity as a mode in relationships which can underpin distance in some relationships and be mobilised as a basis of proximity in others. This discussion will pave the way to further analysis of migrants' sociality on a broader scale. The key idea here will be focusing on migrant relationships *per se* as a means to develop a more balanced understanding of migrant sociality in a super-diverse city. This emphasis on actual relationships between migrant subjects is intended to avoid the clumsy reifications of 'ethnic communities' and superficial abstractions that beset some discourse on transnational links. Nevertheless, this analysis does maintain a degree of openness to the insights afforded by more nuanced calibrations of ethnic and transnational socialities, and does not abandon these approaches out of hand. Finally, the arguments in this and previous chapters serve to introduce and conceptualise friendship as a useful and nuanced way of analysing migrant sociality.

Ethnicity and migration

Ethnicity plays an important role in migration research (Eriksen 2002; Fenton 2010). Earlier sociological and anthropological thought suggested that ethnicity as a social and political force would gradually disappear and eventually be replaced by more comprehensive identities and attachments with the development of the modern world. The second half of the 20th century demonstrated that ethnic attachments would not decline as forces of segregation and cohesion. Migrants were described as usually combining the strategies of both assimilation and ethnic incorporation as parts of the integration process (Eriksen 2002: 124).

In current scholarship, ethnicity is usually presented through various social processes by which ethnic identities and boundaries are reproduced and transformed, and by which individuals form and act as ethnic groups (Cornell and Hartmann 2007). Ethnic ties are described as including a reference to the unity of people of common blood or descent. The key point here is that since Max Weber's intervention, ethnicity is no longer understood as denoting actual commonality of descent, but rather people's mutual belief in it (1968 cited in Cornell and Hartmann 2007: 17). Ethnicity is often based upon ideas of shared culture and an array of public and private identities which coalesce around these ideas (Fenton 2010: 12, 187). The other characteristic of ethnicity is people's self-consciousness as a group, or seeing themselves as distinct from other groups on the grounds of ethnic features. The very definition of a group and its self-consciousness can be grounded in the intertwining processes of that group's self-identification as well as its categorisation by outsiders (Jenkins 2008). This points to an understanding of ethnicity as a relational construct, that is, an 'aspect of social relationship between persons who consider themselves as essentially distinctive from members of other groups of whom they are aware and with whom they enter into relationships' (Eriksen 2002: 12). 'Us' and 'them' are distinguished 'on the basis of the claim we make that "we" share something that "they" do not' (Cornell and Hartmann 2007: 20), therefore these constructs exist in a context that has to include the simultaneous existence of the 'other'.

Most contemporary writers on ethnicity assume a social constructivist approach to this phenomenon (Cornell and Hartmann 2007; Fenton 2010; Jenkins 2008). Within this approach ethnic and racial identities are seen as 'highly variable and contingent products of an ongoing interaction between, on the one hand, the circumstances groups encounter—including the conceptions and actions of outsiders—and, on the other, the actions and conceptions of group members—of insiders. It makes groups active agents in the making and remaking of their own identities, and it views construction not as a one-time event, but as continuous and historical' (Cornell and Hartmann 2007: 87). Ethnicity, thus, is considered to be a social construction of descent and culture, and the social mobilisation of both these social constructions and the meanings of classification systems built around them (Fenton 2010: 3). It is not a property of a group, but a relational and situational communication of differences and similarities, whenever these are thought to be relevant for group formation. Ethnic groups themselves are not fixed entities, and perceptions of these as rigid and clearly bounded (or 'groupism', in Brubaker's (2004) terms) are widely criticised (Eriksen 2002).

Internal and external factors contribute to the shaping of ethnicity (Eriksen 2002). Cornell and Hartmann (2007: 13) note that research on ethnicity has to understand 'both how people interpret and negotiate their lives in ethnic or racial ways and how larger historical and social forces organise the arenas and terms in which those people act, encouraging or discouraging the interpretations they make, facilitating some forms of organisation and action and hindering others'. Ethnic identities and boundaries are created in the processes of interaction between contexts and actions. The key areas where ethnicity's meaningfulness is developed may be broadly defined as sets of economic and political conditions (Fenton 2010: 140). These 'construction sites', in Cornell and Hartmann's (2007: 170) terms, can include politics, labour markets, residential space, social institutions, culture, and daily experience. At the same time, people bring their own characteristics into these processes: their pre-existing identities, internal and external relationships, internal differentiations, various combinations of types of capital, and symbolic repertoires (Cornell and Hartmann 2007: 211). Ethnicity can be understood both through the 'cultural stuff' (Barth 1969 cited in Fenton, 2010) and its social relevance in changing contexts (Eriksen 2002: 138; Fenton 2010).

The construction of ethnicity involves assumptions about classifications of people and their group relationships. Classifications include internal assertions about a group and external assignments of categories, or internal and external definitions (Brubaker 2004: 65; Jenkins 2008: 55). These processes are closely interrelated: categories may be defined by others and filled with their own content within a group. Ethnic ideologies can also be used to justify social hierarchies, in addition to other criteria like gender, class, and age (although researchers agree that racial relations are more likely to be hierarchical, exploitative, or conflictual (Cornell and Hartmann 2007; Jenkins 2008)). These processes of ethnic categorisation are crucial to how ethnic identification works, and power relations are often involved. It is in the interactional process across the boundary between 'us' and 'them', that is, 'in the meeting of internal and external definition that identity, whether collective or individual, is created' (Jenkins 2008: 55). Ethnic identification can mean different things for different people and be of different significance, and therefore encompasses the complexity and variability in the manifestations, functioning, and significance of ethnicity.

Brubaker (2004: 11) underlines the necessity of conceptualising ethnicity in 'relational, processual, dynamic, eventful and disaggregated terms'. Following Brubaker, this study regards ethnicity as a mode of belonging which emerges when certain meaningfulness is assigned to particular cultural commonalities between people, and is used to justify a distance from those who do not seem to possess this 'cultural stuff'. The issue of primary importance for this work is the relational aspect of ethnicity, which implies the often simultaneous malleability of ethnic boundaries and the rigidity of concerns about the potentially ethnic determinants of social groups' qualities. Some migration research asserts that ethnicity keeps being an important aspect of identity for contemporary migrants; moreover, it has been argued that transnational practices and ethnic identification are not necessarily mutually exclusive (Levitt and Glick Schiller 2004; Van Bochove et al. 2010; Van Bochove 2012). Eriksen (2002: 155) writes about the emergence of collective identity among minorities 'which is neither diasporic nor transnational nor ethnic, but defined through locality and the fact of exclusion from [...] majority society'. This is why the focus of this work is on the informal relationships of migrants—with compatriots and other Londoners, both local and transnational, and seen through the prism of life in London. The perceived meanings of ethnicity often play a role in the development of particular attitudes and relationships, as well as the emergence of certain groups among migrants. Ethnicity is constantly in the process of negotiation, which makes the sociality of migrants not necessarily 'ethnic', and the idea of a singular migrant community irrelevant. Rather than exploring mere 'ethnic' group relationships, it would make sense to focus on migrants' informal relationships, in a manner that considers the possible dynamics of the role that ethnicity can play in a local London context and, perhaps more importantly, concentrate on the moments when these relationships become perceived as being devoid of ethnic, cultural, or linguistic underpinnings.

Social relationships amongst migrants

Cohen (2008: 173) argues that social relationships in a diaspora are based on the 'bonds of language, religion, culture and a sense of a common history and perhaps a common fate' that give these relationships an affective and intimate quality. For traditional diaspora members, according to this view, the ethnicity and community of compatriots abroad seem to be the most important factors which provide cohesion. The emergence of transnationalism, no matter how controversial it may be, incorporates the increased possibilities of belonging to different communities simultaneously. The ways in which contemporary migrants form groups have become more diverse, principally because they have more opportunities to be connected, while there is also a great variety in the numbers and strengths of such connections.

Increased cross-border activity and communication is realised through migrants' participation in the social networks of relatives, friends, acquaintances and colleagues Special attention in transnationalism studies has been paid to the networks of kin that work across the boundaries of nation-states (Glick Schiller et al. 1995). These family networks provide possibilities for survival and social mobility. Less attention is paid to other kinds of social networks. Conradson and Latham (2005a) argue that friendship amongst New Zealand migrants in London plays a central role in organising and giving content to their mobility, emphasising how these bonds shape people's movements. This study considers friendship networks highly relevant for research on mobility and transnationalism because they have important affective qualities, are not limited by bonds of kinship or neighbourhood (Conradson and Latham 2005a;

Wellman *et al.* 1988, 1990, 2001), and are 'more fluid and less spatially bounded' (Bunnell *et al.* 2012). As well, they cannot be simply reduced or equated to ethnic or national ties. At the same time, these are relationships that work across space and time, and inform much contemporary migration. Within contemporary migration scholarship, and studies focusing on transnationalism or ethnicity in particular, the topic of friendship has gradually started to receive mention as a separate kind of relationship (Bunnell et al. 2012; Conradson and Latham 2005a; Kennedy 2004; Morosanu 2013a; Reynolds 2007; Ryan 2011; Schlueter 2012; Tsujimoto 2014; Walsh 2009).

Social networks have always played a crucial role in migrants' lives, primarily because of all the tangible and intangible support they provide to migrants. Migration spreads through social networks, which are 'the sets of cross-border interpersonal ties connecting migrants, return migrants and nonmigrants through kinship, friendship and attachment to a shared place of origin' (Levitt, 2001: 8). Levitt asserts: when a network is settled, it becomes more likely that additional migration will occur as there is a group of 'experts' already in the receiving country to serve as newcomers' guides. However, social networks may weaken when there are no new arrivals reinforcing them or when migrants transfer their economic and political loyalties to the communities that receive them. Smith (2001: 170) calls transnational communities 'translocality-based structures of cultural production and social reproduction'. Networks of migrants are a cultural medium for the circulation of symbolic and material capital across borders. Practices embodied in historically specific, culturally constituted social relations connect social networks located in more than one national territory.

According to Levitt (2001: 26), migrants who are incorporated insecurely into the labour market find it easier to maintain a transnational lifestyle, as the new conditions seem to be unstable. It encourages them to keep connected with their relatives (friends, colleagues, employers) in their country of origin; at the same time, economic instability can also be a reason for keeping closer contacts with other migrants, as the migrant community can provide a more familiar environment. Portes (2000: 257) characterises migrant social networks as, firstly, being simultaneously dense and extended over physical distances; secondly, as tending to 'generate solidarity by virtue of generalised uncertainty'. At the same time, it is not just economic insecurity that brings people together; reducing networks and relationships to class would significantly limit the focus of migration scholarship. Indeed, the focus on 'middling' migrants is not uncommon for studies of migration and friendship (Conradson and Latham 2005a; Kennedy 2004; Walsh 2009). Conradson and Latham (2005b: 287) point to the need to study global mobility not just through the economic structures driving migration, but also consider the role played by 'a complex set of personal motivations, amongst which financial considerations are not necessarily primary'.

While speaking about migrants and their social networks as communities, special care should be taken so that the term 'community', when used in a general context, is used no more than as a heuristic device. Not all members of the presumed 'community' feel solidarity toward one another (Levitt 2001: 13). Social groups are characterised by divisiveness and hierarchical factors, increasingly so in conditions of super-diversity. Any migrant group, whether transnational or not, involves a variety of relationships and attitudes amongst its members. Therefore supposing that migrant communities are by definition bound together risks failing to apprehend the complexity of those social relations that position migrants in different ways within the social spaces of the host and home countries, and in the spaces in between.

Since the 2004 EU accession there has been a sizeable migration from the then new EU states to the UK. Relatively recently, this burgeoning migration has been the focus of a strand of migration research. These works are of crucial importance for this study, and have significantly enriched UK migration scholarship; importantly, they have presented some analyses that can be extended to a broader range of cases beyond EU East Europeans. This research takes inspiration from those studies that have focused on social networks and relationships, and which have tackled these as dynamic, diverse and controversial areas, often not limiting their focus to compatriots or co-ethnics. Many of these recent works distinguish ethnic ties from social connectivity and critically disentangle the nuanced character of ethnicity as well as the different strengths, uses and values of social ties (Datta and Brickell 2009; Garapich 2012; Morosanu 2013a, 2013b; Ryan et al. 2008; Ryan 2011; White and Ryan 2008). Relationships with 'others' are an important part of this discourse. Datta (2009) looks at East European construction workers and their interaction with 'others' in London, and regards their cosmopolitanisms as 'neither a cultural project, nor just a survival strategy, but a complex mixture of cultural, ordinary, banal, coerced, and globalised cosmopolitanisms that are enacted under different spatial circumstances of interaction, subjective positioning, and physical proximity'. Louise Ryan, who in her study of Polish migrants uses the concepts of social capital, bonding and bridging ties, [5] criticises the oversimplification in the use of these concepts that results in using ethnicity as a means of distinction between types of relationships. She calls for paying more attention to the 'the relationship between the actors, their relative social location, and

---

[5] Ryan introduces the prevailing understanding of the two types of ties as follows: 'bonding involves close ties with 'people like us' while bridging involves links beyond 'group cleavages'' (Ryan 2011: 707) . She concludes her paper with suggestions to refine the understanding of the concepts: 'both bonding and bridging capital appear to have quite complex relationships to ethnicity. Rather than attempting to differentiate bonding and bridging on the basis of how similar or dissimilar people are, it is more useful to think about the nature of the relationship and the resources available. Bonding may involve close relationships based on emotional intimacy while bridging may result in flows of information, advice or knowledge but without intimacy' (Ryan 2011: 721).

their available and realisable resources' (Ryan 2011: 707). Laura Morosanu, who focuses on Romanians in London, underlines the complications of sustaining ties both 'here' and 'there', and presents a fragmented version of migrant social lives in order to support her argument that the role of ethnicity should not be overestimated. In writing about close and lasting connections which contradict migrants' negative generalisations about their home country and co-ethnics, Morosanu explores the idea of 'soul friendships' which are 'based on long-term engagement, frequent interaction, shared experiences and affectivity, and have minimal ethnic grounding, showing that the role of ethnicity should not be readily assumed' (Morosanu 2013a: 353).

Social networks and relationships are created and sustained across borders by migrants when they arrive in a country, transplanted from their country of origin and re-established in a new place of residence. Not everyone engages in the same networks to the same degree and such relationships can change over time. In addition, the sociality of migrants does not have to be and is not directed only at compatriots. This study supports a more refined strategy for researching contemporary migration and transnationalism, and seeks to avoid conceptualising migrants as homogeneously transnational groups that rely on kinship connections. This means taking into account that neither an overbearing focus on transnational connectivity or ethnic ties can be entirely helpful if we are to understand the diversity and complexity of migrant social connections. As Morosanu (2010) asserts, such an understanding of migrant networks and interactions is crucial for super-diverse societies.

Friendship is a particular kind of relationship that has started to receive attention in migration literature and helped provide useful insights into relationships that are both local and spatially distanciated. The focus on friendship responds to the need for balanced and detailed research of the dynamics and functioning of migrants' social networks, as well as the need to adequately address the increasingly heterogeneous character of contemporary migration. Simply put, studying migrants' social networks in a detailed way requires that we reach beyond migrants' relationships with their kin and compatriots and turn to those which they maintain with other people. In the subsequent section, the importance of migrants' informal relationships in a super-diverse city is addressed, particularly with regard to how informal relationships are more complex and nuanced than the ideas of communities based upon ethnicity or transnational ties.

The nature of friendship

Friendship remains a relatively marginal concept in the social sciences (Bunnell et al. 2012). Since the development of impersonal market relations and bureaucratic mechanisms in Western Europe, as noted by Kharkhordin (2009), friendship has been largely regarded as a relationship reduced to the private sphere and to a small number of individual connections, which has resulted in making this concept a less common object for the social sciences. In particular, migration research has addressed different topics concerning social connectivity—social capital, cohesion, ties, and networks (Cheong et al. 2007; Hall 2011; Putnam 2007; Ryan et al. 2008; Soehl and Waldinger 2010; White and Ryan 2008), but friendship rarely comes up as a separate research focus (Bunnell et al. 2012; Conradson and Latham 2005a; Kennedy 2004). Being closely related to those aspects of sociality which pertain to social capital, cohesion and networks, friendship emerges as a particular kind of relationship that has a strong but understudied impact on the lives of mobile individuals and their communities.

In research into the attributes of sociality, the issue of instrumentality is often central. The works of Durkheim and Tönnies describe the opposition of societies with organic and mechanic solidarity, or

Gemeinschaft and *Gesellschaft,* where the former represent 'traditional' forms of interpersonal relationships, and the latter suggest rationalised, exchange-like relationships (Calhoun *et al.* 2005). In contrast to this treatment of instrumentality, Simmel (1949: 54) regarded sociability as a largely idealistic process, an 'art or play form of association, related to the content and purposes of association in the same way as art is related to reality'.

A strand of more recent research that contributed significantly to the development of social network analysis (Fischer 1977; Wellman et al. 1988, 1990) drew upon social exchange theory and quantitative measurements to suggest that individuals associate with each other because, at a fundamental level, they gain profit from their associations. From this perspective, the anticipation of potential rewards is the underlying basis of attraction for any association. Fischer supports the choice-constraint model as an explanation of how interpersonal relationships are choices made with limited alternatives and resources. However, in this work I advocate an understanding of friendship as a relationship that can neither be reduced to a purely instrumental relationship, nor simply to emotional attachment. Bourdieu (1998) has approached the economic side of sociality, and claimed that while people often describe everyday exchanges as friendship, the act of calling them as such supports a network of the informal exchange of goods and services. Friendship, thus, becomes 'a place where interest, in the narrow sense of the pursuit of equivalence in exchanges, is suspended' (Bourdieu 1998: 65). Participants' mutual suppression of the economic reality of exchange at the heart of friendship is a necessary condition of its existence. Boltanski (2012) adds to this the refusal to exercise critical capacity in regard of the relationship. Boltanski designates this refusal as agape, which can be regarded as analogous to authentic friendship in his works, and can develop when the participants of a relationship do not rely upon the anticipated reaction of their companions, and consciously refuse to calculate the value of the exchanged resources and services. [6] Boltanski and Thévenot (1999: 361) have written about a principle of equivalence which clarifies what people have in common and which is used to justify 'the operation of bringing together different items or different facts' in a dispute, thereby creating connections between such items and facts with underlying criticisms. In the 'ordinary course of common action', then, people use their abilities to calculate in order to criticise. In the affective regime of coordination (which can be used to describe friendship) 'persons actively cooperate in the process of shoving the equivalencies aside in order to render difficult the cumulating and calculation operations which are required to blame and criticise' (Boltanski and Thévenot 1999: 362). In other words, according to this approach, the conscious denial of the pragmatic or exchange-like implications of friendship is authentic friendship.

Unlike kinship, friendships do not exist as a given: they 'require—and may even be defined in terms of—active, ongoing and necessarily reciprocal work' (Bunnell et al. 2012: 494). These relationships provide social support and make up much of the social capital people use to deal with daily life, seizing opportunities or reducing uncertainties. Social networks have also been a common topic for migration research that has stressed their influence on mi-

---

[6] '...in contrast with *philia*, based on the notion of reciprocity [...] *agape* as a gift expects nothing in return, either in the material form of objects or in the immaterial form of requited love. [...] Actors in a state of agape do not model their behaviour on the way they think others will respond to their acts. They do not incorporate in their own acts the anticipated response of the person or persons to whom they are addressing themselves, and thus, in defiance of all modern theories of action, whether they stem from psychology, sociology or economics, they do not envisage the relation to others in the form of a sequence of strike and counter-strikes' (Boltanski 2012: 112). '...if the regime of *agape* is to be maintained, all persons must be inhabited by the same lack of interest in calculation, and all must have access to the same resources, the ones necessary to do the work – on themselves and on others – that ensures the inhibition of the calculating capabilities naturally present in human persons' (Boltanski 2012: 149).

gration-related decisions, particularly with regard to how they provide information, resources and emotional support (Boyd 1989; Ryan 2011). 'Network capital' has been approached in the social sciences as making resources available through interpersonal ties, and includes emotional and material aid, information, companionship, and a sense of belonging (Wellman and Frank 2001). The constructive role of friendship on a structural level has also received some critical discussion. Pahl mentioned the importance of informal solidarity based on friendship, and claimed that it can help support an increasingly fragmented social structure (Pahl 2000: 11). In a similar vein, Kharkhordin (2009: 12) argues that in the times of social uncertainty and anomie after the break-up of the Soviet Union, it was friendship that, as a widespread and naturally self-reproducing resource, helped Russia recover from social collapse, and held the disintegrating society together. Pahl linked together large-scale social factors with such small-scale interpersonal relationships as friendship: 'The social form of friendship must be related to the encapsulating social formation of the society as a whole. It affects the way we develop the personal, which may be more or less constricted by wider structures and processes' (Pahl 2000: 64). At the same time, not all community ties have been shown to be supportive (Wellman et al. 1988, 1990; Wellman and Frank 2001); a conclusion which has been empirically demonstrated by migration research (Hellerman 2006; Menjívar 2000; Morosanu 2013a; Ryan et al. 2008).

These ideas of instrumentality and social capital in relationships are unavoidably connected with debates over space, particularly when an analysis seeks to explore migrants' cross-border relationships. As already noted, critical attention to kinship in transnational studies, the tendency to look at migrant social networks through the lens of ethnic communities, and the focus on 'community' and 'neighbourhood' in the social sciences (Bunnell et al. 2012) have prompted some researchers to seek a path beyond conventional iterations of cross-border connectivity, ethnicity and communities, and approach the problem of social relationships per se. Wellman in his studies on East York (Wellman et al. 1988, 1990; Wellman and Frank 2001) argues for focusing on all members of a network and not only neighbours or kin. He claims that communities as networks do not have to be seen as necessarily bounded by place (neighbourhood) or solidarity groups (kinfolk). He criticises 'neighbourhood chauvinism', emphasises that that 'community is where you find it' (Wellman et al., 1988: 130), and underlines the importance of studying social structure and social linkages, for 'social sentiments and spatial distribution hold important, but secondary positions' (Wellman 1979: 1202). Wellman argues for a focus on a 'personal community network', that is, a person's set of active community ties which are usually socially diverse, spatially disperse, and sparsely knit (Wellman and Wortley 1990). Pahl (2000), too, underlined a growing centrality of personal communities as opposed to geographical or work-based communities in contemporary Western societies. These personal communities may be geographically scattered and may change substantially as people move through their life-course. [7] Research on migrant networks suggests going beyond studies of social capital within communities and local neighbourhoods, and argues that more attention be paid to the dynamic, diverse and spatially dispersed character of migrants' social networks—in other words, to focus on the actual relationships of migrants (Ryan et al. 2008; Ryan 2011; Morosanu 2010).

As already stated, the primary relationship with which this study concerns itself is friendship. Given the above discussion over the dangers of totalising applications of 'global' theoretical constructs to actual social phenomena in particular contexts, it is important to incorporate a discussion of the particularities of friendship in Russia

---

[7] However, he also noted that despite frequent visits, phone calls, emails, and letters, there still can be no substitute for geographical propinquity (Pahl 2000: 8).

and the former Soviet Union to the present critique of relationships. Bunnell et al. (2012: 492) warn that the meanings attached to friendship take on different connotations in different sociocultural contexts. It seems logical to attend to the particularities of friendship in Russia and the former Soviet Union, where most of the members of the contemporary Russian-speaking population of London were born and brought up. In the next section, I will present a brief overview of the roots of Soviet understandings of friendship. Then, having established friendship as a specific mode of social interaction, it may be transplanted from migrants' home countries and guide the ways in which migrants in London can form meaningful social relationships.

(post) Soviet friendship

Research on the social role of friendship in the Soviet Union is quite scarce. Shlapentokh (1989: 171; 1984: 214) has pointed out that in official Soviet ideology friendship never had a significant social value. The value of collectivism was not identified with that of friendship, primarily because the collective implies interactions of many people, while friendship usually involves dyadic and personal relations. While the collective relied on the existence of external control, friendship, in contrast, rejected the idea of any intervention (Shlapentokh 1984: 214). In this respect, the Soviet mass media used the term with specifically positive connotations, applying it to a macro level of friendship between peoples or classes, rather than to private relationships. Even when personal friendship emerged as a topic, it was usually framed in the context of the military or workplace relations, thereby implying its benefit for society or the state, but not for the individuals concerned. Shlapentokh parallels this with the ideas of dystopian writers such as Zamiatin and Orwell, who considered friendship in a totalitarian society an obstacle to the domination of the state over the individual. In his research on sociality in the Soviet Union, Kharkhordin (1999, 2009) also underlines that friendship was never an official Soviet value like the 'kollektiv', which was held to be superior in official discourse. Kollektiv was a constructed, culturally specific phenomenon which existed almost exclusively in Soviet society, and was generally defined as a group of people united by a common goal and a common activity. Mutual surveillance spanned the collectives: Soviet tourists always travelled abroad in groups (at least one member of which was necessarily pursuing official surveillance) and could not walk around in a Western city alone, but only in groups of three or more (Kharkhordin 1999: 110). Friendship, thus, became 'an institution against the state' (Shlapentokh 1984: 213). It helped to form informal social networks that were subversive of the Soviet system of collective surveillance and discipline (Kharkhordin 2009: 13).

The fact that official Soviet media never praised personal friendship is not, however, tantamount to stating that it did not exist. Informal relationships in small networks were an important part of everyday life in the Soviet Union. In this respect, friendship in Soviet society had a number of functions. Friends could be relied upon as an alternative source of information beyond that provided in the state's officially sanctioned discourse. For example, people would share information they had heard on a foreign radio. Such an exchange could happen only when people trusted each other. Friends could be trusted in an emergency situation and would not betray an individual even under the threat of persecution. They also provided help in everyday practices of 'beating the system': procuring scarce or unobtainable goods, helping with access to services, and supporting the 'second economy' in general—the unofficial system of distributing goods and services parallel to the official economy (Shlapentokh 1989: 174). Shlapentokh also notes 'the overwhelming friendship and hospitality expressed in the so-called kitchen culture. The conviviality and warmth invariably found there was in marked contrast to the stultifying formality and hypocrisy of public life' (Shlapentokh 1989 cited in Pahl, 2000: 156).

The moral foundations of late Soviet friendship have received some discussion in critical literature. Kon (1987) wrote that mature friendship satisfies two of an individual's basic needs: to trust another person unconditionally and to talk about one's problems. Shlapentokh (1989: 174) describes a friend as an individual 'to whom you can pour out your soul, who recognises your virtues and is tolerant of your weaknesses, who is your advisor in intimate spheres of life, and with whom it is pleasant to spend your leisure time'. Unconditional trust and a chance to confide and discuss personal problems at any time—these features made mature Soviet friendship an unofficial moral value. Similarly to what has been written earlier in this chapter on instrumentality in social relationships, friendship as an unconditional relationship is supposed to be free from any rational calculations: 'as a moral relationship, friendship emerges only after the interpersonal tie stops being considered as a pure expression of emotional attraction, social duty, or the result of a rational calculation. Rituals of attraction, or calculation do not cease to exist and do not lose their autonomous meaning. But now, they conform to higher moral considerations, combined with the concepts of obligation and virtue. From now on, "real friendship" becomes a model [...] which represents such personal constants as selectivity, individuality, loyalty, [and] independence from the situational considerations' (Kon 1987: 107). Friendship, then, becomes an exercise in 'active forgetting' (Kharkhordin 2009: 20), which is similar to Boltanski's reflections on how subjects do not necessarily exercise their capacity for criticism in a relationship. Again, there are references to a 'real' and 'authentic' friendship that is supposed to comply with these moral requirements.

As Kharkhordin claims, Soviet friendship created a space for individualisation, getting to know one's own personality and the formation of individual identity, because friends offered a space for existentially meaningful communication (2009: 14). He underlines that the function of friendship did not disappear in the 1990s, when the repressive abilities of the state decreased. In this respect, he regards Russian friendship as being not very dependent upon the condition of state institutions. With the transformation of elements of Soviet society during this period, friendship networks remained a significant constitutive element of the functioning of post-Soviet society.

If friendship was formed in conditions of repressive politics, economic and informational scarcity, and in opposition to the official valorisation of the collective, it became a relationship of a special quality. The status of a friend was not something that could be ascribed, but was rather an achievement that required a significant effort, as it took some time to find out if one could really trust a particular person (Kharkhordin 2009: 13; Shlapentokh 1984: 244). A moving example provided by Shlapentokh (1984: 233-236) from his own personal experiences (but which he also addressed with the analytical rigour of a social scientist) concerns his friends' reactions when they became aware of his intention to leave the Soviet Union. As soon as he made a decision to leave in 1979, his formal status in society changed. A renowned sociologist, he was placed by the state in a kind of demoralising vacuum, which was common for would-be emigrants at that time. [8] He made a list of his friends and

---

8   Shlapentokh (1984: 233) writes: 'After my decision to leave the Soviet Union, my status in society changed drastically. Previously a well-known Soviet sociologist and Senior Fellow in the prestigious Sociological Institute of the Academy of Science in Moscow, I enjoyed relatively high status in the scientific community, even if my status was higher among intellectuals than officials. After I applied for an exit visa, however, my status was radically altered.
[...] we can look at a picture of the typical situation facing a scholar who has chosen to emigrate. Quickly the scholar will be 1) relieved of all teaching activities; 2) have his graduate students transferred to other supervisors; 3) be deprived of the possibility of publishing articles and books, and have all those in print destroyed; 4) have all his books removed from libraries; 5) have all invitations to participate in conferences and seminars cancelled; 6) be excluded from all councils and other bodies of which he is a member; 7) in some cases, also be deprived of scholarly titles and degrees; 8) in many cases, be fired without any prospect of finding another job; 9) have his children expelled from universities or colleges; 10) face special meetings in the institute, organized to make public denunciation of this antipatriotic act, with orchestrated speeches made by colleagues; and so on.

acquaintances and tried to measure the change in their attitudes towards him. He found that despite the pressure of the authorities and possible reputational risks posed by maintaining the relationship, the majority of these people behaved 'with a distinct lack of obedience to the regime'. His closest friends did not turn their backs and stop communication with him, and many even increased their contact with him. He concludes that friendship turned out to be the strongest value, as people were willing to sacrifice other values such as their reputation for the sake of their relationship.

Shlapentokh's emphasis on friendship's moral dimension allows to regard it as a kind of shelter from external threats. Shlapentokh (1989: 218) wrote that: 'all other things equal, the lower the sense of security among people and the weaker their confidence in the future, the more intense and vital are interpersonal relationships. This can be demonstrated by the closeness of relations among those belonging to an oppressed minority as compared to those of a dominant majority'. Shlapentokh's argument can be used to bridge experiences of migration and the practices and dynamics of friendship. This study has argued that contemporary migration is not an easy route for many individuals, despite the world being globalised and increasingly interconnected. Friendship can therefore provide an opportunity to protect oneself from the tensions and insecurities that beset migrant experience, and provide necessary network capital through social support. At the same time, however, the flip side of such images of friendship as a moral but also subversive practice is its potential to increase social divisions, exclusive relationships, mistrust, and the fragmentation of other social ties. Friendship among post-Soviet migrants, then, could potentially become racialised by assigning to it values that may distinguish it from other relationships, or, crucially, relationships with 'others', and

---

[...] each act of harassment also signals to friends, colleagues, and acquaintances that the maintenance of good relations with the applicant for the visa would be regarded as unloyal behaviour, with possible negative consequences for those who choose to ignore these warnings'.

therefore reinforce divisions. However, it also provides space for the transgression of such distinctions, and can be regarded as opening up possibilities for the development of 'everyday cosmopolitanism' in practice, similar to that which Datta (2009: 367) describes as 'produced from [migrants'] transnational histories, nationalistic notions of gender, race, and ethnicity, and subjective positions of power that are operationalised in and through the everyday places in a global city'.

Late Soviet friendship presents itself as a relatively small-scale, moral, consciously calculation-free and informal relationship that can have subversive qualities in its opposing other groups and their potential influence to the migrant subject, and is therefore potentially ambiguous in terms of its supportive and divisive qualities. It was understood and practiced as a relationship which had to pass the test of time in order to develop trust. This historical and sociocultural background of sociality can inform the lives of migrants, their relationships with each other, local and cross-border connections, and communication with compatriots and non-Russian-speaking Londoners.

Conclusions

Rather than starting this analysis with the concerns of transnational connectivity or ethnic communities or groups, this chapter has suggested approaching migrant sociality through analysing the actual relationships that people develop, sustain or cut off while living as migrants, be it locally or transnationally, with co-ethnics or 'others'. The relational aspects of ethnicity are underlined here, while I also emphasise that its perceived meanings are subject to negotiation, thus making migrant sociality not necessarily ethnic and the idea of a singular migrant community irrelevant. The focus on the informal relationships of migrants can take into account the possible dynamics and importance of the role that ethnicity might play for migrants in London; but equally, it should remain open to the moments when these relationships are perceived as being devoid of ethnic, cultural, or linguistic underpinnings.

The social networks created by migrants are sustained across borders after subjects arrive in a country, transplanted from their country of origin and establish themselves in a new place of residence. These networks are an important source of social support and social capital. However, engagement into informal relationships is dynamic and may change over time. In addition, the sociality of migrants is not necessarily directed only at compatriots. Besides, concentrating on the positive characteristics of social networks should not mean neglecting the negative or destructive impacts that some relationships and networks have on migrant lives. A more refined strategy of researching contemporary migration would mean taking into account that neither focus on transnational connectivity nor ethnic ties can be entirely helpful in attempts to understand the diversity and complexity of migrant social connections.

Friendship, previously a relatively marginal topic, has started to receive mention in migration literature as a particular kind of relationship, and helped provide useful insights into the patterns of relationships across space and time. The focus on friendship responds to the need for balanced and detailed research on the dynamics and functioning of migrants' social networks, and consideration of the increasingly heterogeneous character of contemporary migration. If we are to study migrants' social networks, we must reach beyond relations with kin and compatriots and address migrants' relationships with other people. Any resulting insights from this approach can contribute to our understanding of social processes in the super-diverse city and globalised world beyond. In the particular empirical case of post-Soviet Russian-speaking migrants in London, it also allows us to explore the ambiguous supportive and divisive legacy of late Soviet friendship: a small-scale, moral, deeply trusting and informal relationship that is consciously free of calculation and potentially has subversive qualities which may serve to juxtapose and divide. This historical and sociocultural background of sociality can inform the lives of migrants, their relationships with each other, local and cross-border connections, as well as their communication with compatriots and non-Russian-speaking Londoners.

I argue here that friendship networks are relevant for migration research because they have important affective qualities, are not limited by bonds of kinship or neighbourhood, are relatively flexible, and are not tied to a locality. In addition, they cannot be simply reduced or equated to ethnic or national ties, as demonstrated by some of the most recent studies on East European migrants in London. The focus on friendship will facilitate a critique of the development and proliferation of migrants' personal networks that considers the dynamics of their attitudes towards compatriots and 'others'; thus avoiding the risk of taking for granted the perceptions of a particular migrant community, and approaching their wider set of significant relationships and networks without discarding their transnationality or ethnicity.

Chapter 3
Localising friends

The two previous theoretical chapters are consistent with the growing body of migration research which argues that the diversity of migrant populations and the variety of their social ties must be addressed. As already noted, the theoretical paradigm advanced here is a means of going beyond reductive and essentialised iterations of ethnicity and diffuse treatments of transnationalism. The focus on migrants' social relationships per se does not discard questions of ethnicity or transnationalism, and is intended to develop a more balanced understanding of migrant sociality in a super-diverse city; that is, an understanding which is attentive to relationships' affective dynamics within and across spatial boundaries, and the limitations of conceptualisations of ethnicity, national ties, kinship or locality in migrant social life. This and the following chapters provide an empirical analysis of friendship. I suggested that friendships, or, rather, 'real' friendships may be perceived as outstanding relationships. It has also been emphasised that not only the supportive potential of friendships, but also their possibly divisive and exclusive features should be an important factor for consideration. Also, I suggested that the historical and sociocultural legacy of late Soviet friendship can inform the lives of migrants, their relationships with each other, local and cross-border connections, and communication with compatriots and non-Russian-speaking Londoners. It is precisely this focus on their networks that permits the reappraisal of the place of ethnic ties and transnationalism within friendly relationships.

By way of a beginning this work's empirical[9] analysis, I will demonstrate how Russian-speakers establish, re-establish and maintain

---

9   Methodologically, this research was based upon half a year of participant observation in a Russian bar and 35 semi-structured interviews with migrants, which took place from 2009-2011. These methods were chosen as the most

their social networks and friendships while living in London, and how their friendships are entangled with places. More precisely, I will discuss what happens when Russian-speakers meet each other in the city, how and why personal contact can be prompted (or not), and how the image of 'Russian friendship' feeds into social and spatial distances and proximities.

'It just happens'

Viktor[10] is a tall, deep-chested guy with a shaved head and tunnel piercings in his ears. He is driving his car, playing with his iPhone, smoking and constantly talking to strangers outside—other drivers and pedestrians. The car stops at a red light, Viktor turns his head to the right just to say cheerfully to another driver: 'Hey man, how are you, you all right?' The guy mumbles something; Viktor contentedly nods and hits the accelerator.

---

appropriate for studying a relatively new, small, growing, socially diverse, and spatially disperse part of the migrant population of London that is not available for large-scale structured research, and is not well represented in British migration literature. The fieldwork process and dynamics correspond with the ideas of studying friendship of mostly 'middling' Russian-speaking migrants by observing and talking about their everyday lives, as a localised set of informal relationships that have both local and distanciated origins. This was meant to help understand how migrants shape and sustain their social networks, how they build relationships across the borders and locally, and how they may find themselves incorporated into super-diversity. The time spent in close communication with my informants also developed my critical awareness of the ambiguous relationships of these people. In the course of the study, the ideas of the continuity existing between different kinds of informal relationships of migrants were gradually developed. As a result, I could approach migrants as agents of different sets of relationships: as members of social networks, as individuals engaging in relationships of different degrees of closeness, and as participants of a wider set of urban social relationships within London's diverse population. These research strategies complemented each other and helped picturing the complex and multi-layered patterns of migrant sociality. A more detailed reflection on the methodological and ethical challenges of this ethnographic study can be found here: Malyutina (2012), Malyutina (2014).

10 All names have been changed to preserve anonymity. Any other potentially personally identifying details have been removed.

Viktor depicts himself as an extremely sociable person who cannot live without communication and attention, always actively interacting with the people around him.

> Viktor: I might even not be able to speak someone's language, but even if they do not speak English, we will find common language. If they want to understand, we will be able to have a talk. 'Tienes ojos bonitos', I can say something in Spanish. A couple of good phrases, like this 'you have beautiful eyes'.

Viktor is 21 years old; he came to London from Kyiv, Ukraine, over two years ago. He is a driver in a car hire service and lives in Hackney, East London. He came to London to join his father. 'And then, if not London, where else would I go?' rhetorically questions Viktor. The father is not his only relative residing in London: his uncle and his son, Viktor's cousin, three years his junior, are here, too; as well as his godfather with a wife and two children, with whom Viktor has very warm relations.

Getting acquainted with people is not difficult for him. The constitution of his personal networks is rather mixed, with Russian-speakers prevailing. He used to have two separate phones for Russian- and non-Russian-speakers; there were 480 contacts in the former. Viktor started meeting Russian-speakers initially through his cousin who introduced him to his friends, visiting the occasional informal gatherings of Russian-speaking youth.

> Viktor: I started hanging out with people [*tusovatsya*], and the core of my network concentrated around my cousin, because they were the people he knew. Then gradually I met more and more people. But I am very sociable, I told you. I always engage into conversations with people, and people stick to me—and I enjoy it.

Some of his acquaintances were initiated by rather pragmatic motivations, based on some small services and reciprocity. As Viktor is a driver, several times he was asked to help somebody with transportation. In most of these cases, Viktor's network of contacts expanded and developed through the channels of already existing acquaintances. They introduced new people to him, facilitating their communication in informal circumstances, passed his contact information to others if recommending his services to them. At the same time, it is common for Viktor to start new acquaintances from scratch, which usually happens in the street or in public places.

> *Viktor:* Sure you can recognise a Russian. It happened many times to me. Let's say, a person is walking down the street, I address him in Russian...I can see that he is a Russian-speaker, don't know how, but I can see through him. I start talking to him straight away. He is shocked. And that's it, we begin a conversation. [...] It is so common for me. I often talk to [Russian] girls in the centre like that. Why not? I'm driving my car, see a couple of young pretty girls—why not approach then and say something nice? They are flattered, and you are pleased. And then again, something might come out of that...

Viktor does not have time to cook at home, so he eats out almost all the time. Sometimes he drops by a small café between Chiswick and Hammersmith. The place is officially Italian, but the owners are Ukrainian and Viktor's old friends. He met the owner Lyova through his other friend, and since then he frequents the place, eats borscht and chats with the staff. And it is from Lyova that Viktor hears some gossip about other customers, among them about Vera. Viktor has not met her personally, but knows that she has previously lived in Moscow, has a little son and lives nearby.

Vera is another frequent visitor to this café, a 35-year old Ukrainian-born researcher who lives in a flat in Chiswick with her American husband and two year old son. Her acquaintance with Lyova started not via the channels of personal communication, but rather out of spatial curiosity—one day Vera who enjoys exploring the city just popped in for lunch, and discovered that the place is run by her compatriots.

> *Vera:* I visit them quite often, even if it is just for a cup of coffee. Gradually, they decided to step aside from all these Italian dishes, and now

they are cooking borscht and everything else. Well, Russians frequent them. They do it from under the counter—I mean, they do not have dressed herring [*selyodka pod shuboi*] in the menu. On Tuesdays, they serve cutlets [*kotlety*]...I usually do not eat such fatty food, but I thought—ok, let's try your *kotleta*. Of course, it was delicious...So, I often drop by for a nice chat.

Casual and spontaneous acquaintances with random compatriots, like Viktor's flirting with pretty girls or Vera encountering a Ukrainian owner in a supposedly Italian café, are rather common for the Russian-speaking inhabitants of London. Quite often people initiate such contacts out of a specific curiosity, based on the practical implementation of their skill to recognise people of post-Soviet origin in the streets. That is, for example, how Masha, a 32 year old housewife of Jewish origin from Moscow, and mother of a six months old son, met Vera, Alla and Marina.

> *Masha:* With Vera, I could tell that she was probably Russian, but not so straightforwardly. Because despite she has a Slavic face, she is rather toned down—no bright clothes or aggressive make-up. She could be Polish. I saw her in the market with her son, who had such a cute hat with little ducks. And I asked her where she had bought that hat. I asked in English, and when she replied, she had a very strong accent. I asked—are you Russian? And yes, she was from Moscow. We started talking...

Vera herself gives a similar account of this encounter.

> *Vera*: Yesterday in the market, there was that girl. She looks at Sasha's hat and says—oh, what a pretty hat, where did you get it? I look at her and she seems a bit...strange. It turns out that she is from Moscow, too, and lives in Chiswick as well. I did not express much enthusiasm in the conversation, as it was early morning, and I was quite sleepy... but she was very active. Speaking very adequately, and constantly blah-blah-blah...She even helped me with the buggy. And took my phone number, too.

This way of engagement into communication with Russian-speakers is a sort of *'l'art pour l'art'*, a practice of perfecting one's personal mastery to recognise former compatriots. Marina, a 32 year old Latvian shop assistant who works on a perfume counter in a pharmacy chain in central London, has a habit of recognizing Russian-speaking customers by appearance and occasionally embarrassing them by asking them of their origin in Russian. By doing this, she does not aim to find new friends, but rather seeks entertainment for herself—in fact, she developed relatively lasting relations only with a couple of such acquaintances.

> Marina: As I started working, I learned to see Russians, I started talking to them, and just out of interest, I'm asking them—where are you from? Yes, that's what I do when I hear the customer's accent. [...] Just like that. Not for hanging out with them [*tusovatsya*], it is random guessing. Hit or miss.

Public spaces like parks, markets or public transport are generally common places for such spontaneous interactions to occur. It usually starts with a guess about the post-Soviet origin of the potential interlocutor. Language and accent are another hint when seeking to recognise a Russian-speaker, in addition to certain features of appearance.

> Viktoria: I often notice men's attention on the tube. As if they feel a compatriot in me. Once I was on the tube and there was a man sitting and looking, looking, looking at me. His colleague got off earlier. And then he said rather loudly a couple of phrases in Russian or Ukrainian, for me to pay attention to him… He had his wedding ring on the right hand, so I thought he was Ukrainian. We talked for a while. He said he worked in that area, and I said I was a nanny in that area. It was a non-committal acquaintance, we just exchanged information—where we live, how we live, how much we pay for the rent—technical questions.

The use of certain public spaces implies similarities in people's current life positions and experiences which can promote acquaintance. For example, children and all activities related to looking after them very often facilitate acquaintances, especially among women, leading to their access to particular social networks and friendship groups (Ryan *et al.* 2007: 12). Having kids of similar age provides another common ground for communication, in addition to language and origin. Masha recalls meeting Alla in a children's clinic:

> Masha: There was another mother sitting next to me, and she had a funny baby. And she also had English with a funny accent. I asked where she was from, and she replied she was from Ukraine. Again, the conversation began.

More grown-up kids can be relatively active facilitators of interaction themselves. When Russian-speaking children go to the same school, it is very likely, according to some of the mothers interviewed for this study, that they will become friends themselves and initiate communication between their parents. Moreover, this pattern of socialising, based on children's curiosity and interest to Russian-speakers, expands beyond institutionalised interactions where kids and grown-ups are brought together by a formal purpose like education. Children often feel free to express lively interest in others if they hear them speaking the same language, and don't feel restrained from making the first move and start talking to a person. This is how, for example, Nadezhda, a 45 year old housewife from Russia who lives in Dagenham, met one of her current friends.

> Nadezhda: I met my Ukrainian friend in the park, our children were playing there. Her husband is Nigerian, and the children have darkish skin. It was funny when her daughter heard us speaking Russian, approached us and asked—are you Russian? I say, yes. She says—oh, I am Russian too! And she is a black girl. Then she told her mother, and that is how we met.

Such relatively spontaneous encounters are quite common for respondents, and many of them recall developing a few friendships from these contacts. However, most of such encounters seem to be casual and non-committal, like in Viktoria's quote earlier. In fact, while people generally acknowledge the extensive presence of post-Soviet migrants in the UK, and the high probability of encountering compatriots almost anywhere in the course of their everyday activities, meeting Russian-speakers becomes taken for granted, perceived as one of the usual features of super-diversity. In this regard, acquaintances 'just happen' for many of the respondents as a very natural thing:

> *Karim:* As I told you, I did not aim to find Russians. Both when I came to London and now—I gladly communicate with people of different nationalities, I am interested in them. But it just turned out that way—eventually, very often you do not choose people to be around you, your friends. Really, maybe the reason is that there are so many Russians in the UK, especially students. But it occurred to me that I mainly socialise with Russian-speakers.

Often, contacts are established when people are brought together by a common activity, occupation or hobby; or at events like parties or conferences. Aleksandr, a 23 year old guy from Russia, who has just finished his Bachelors, recalls how he met most of his friends.

> *Aleksandr:* When I was doing my Foundation Course, we had a big company of Russian-speakers. [...] Lucya, for example [his girlfriend]—I met her there, five years ago, at the very first day. There was a meeting, I don't remember, something like an induction. The rest of them—I met them in the classes, we exchanged phone numbers.
>
> *Darya:* Did you just hear a person speaking Russian and talk to him?
>
> *Aleksandr:* Not always, you just can see that the person is Russian, immediately. But speech also matters.

Nadezhda, who has been a big fan of yoga as a spiritual practice, even before moving to London, regularly visits classes. At these classes she met a lot of her current Russian-speaking friends, although they are not aimed only at Russian-speakers. However, this activity has brought her quite a few companions of the same origin. English courses are, too, a common place to find new acquaintances among the people who might share not only origin, but also difficulties with dealing with British culture and strategies of overcoming these difficulties (i.e. attending the courses). In all these experiences of encountering compatriots, though, Russian-ness is not recognised as an ultimate aim of communication. As much as super-diversity is a multiplicity of cultures, languages, ethnicities, and nationalities encountered daily, other Russian-speakers are just another routine part of it. According to research on 'middling' (Conradson and Latham 2005a) or 'lifestyle' (Knowles and Harper 2009) migration patterns, the meaningfulness of being in contact with compatriots is assigned with an almost aesthetic value, being circumstantial and free from obligations to the diasporic community.

Looking for Russian-speakers

At the same time, some migrants articulate a clear intention to look for Russian-speakers. When this does not imply looking for companionship, these intentions may be underpinned by pragmatic motivations, like job matters. One may argue that this applies more to low-skilled migrants, who also may be constrained by a poor command of English. One example is Viktoria, who works as a nanny only for Russian-speaking or mixed families. Another migrant, Seryozha, 24, from Belarus, advertised in Russian language media in London while looking for a casual job, and a Russian mathematician found him through the ad:

> *Seryozha:* I posted an ad in a Russian newspaper about transportation services, and he called. I drove him. Since then, he called a couple of times; he needed a piece of advice on some household issues. Today he called again...

While these migrants were looking for compatriots for the purposes of finding work rather than company, their formal acquaintances often become connected with some informal sociality—Viktoria, for example, became quite close to her employer Vera and her son. Conversely, companionship of FSU migrants can sometimes be sought after as a means of achieving something practical:

> *Nastya:* I registered on one social website, and indicated in my profile that I was from London, not from Bournemouth. And I was deliberately seeking for [Russian] boys from London. Because I already wanted to move to London. Because I was bored in Bournemouth...[...] At the end of the day—if I had not met my former boyfriend via this website and moved to live with him, how the hell would I have moved to London?!...

However, there seem to be many more people who look for Russian-speaking company without pragmatic purposes—rather, for the sake of sociality with compatriots:

> *Yasha:* From the very beginning I had this kind of attitude, I was inclined to get acquainted with Russians, I don't know why. Maybe it is possible to explain it rationally, but my soul was always asking for Russian-speaking socialising.

For some, getting in touch with Russian-speakers happens naturally, as soon as they get to the UK:

> *Vladimir:* I was very active in terms of Russian communication. Basically, it was enough to meet one person in the beginning...[...] I didn't see anything wrong with it. I did not have a desire to assimilate. It seems like you don't really have to! [...] I mean, I am British. But my informal communication network has always been Russian.

The taken-for-grantedness of the presence of FSU migrants in the city is something that migrants acknowledge, and admit that they can choose the degree of involvement in these social networks, depending on the time or the circumstances. Many people's narratives indicate that they find hanging out, talking and discussing sensitive issues, listening and confessing secrets to Russian-speakers easier and more habitual than intimate communication with other Londoners. Therefore, they may aim for companions and friends with a similar outlook (respondents often use the term 'mentality'). Encounters with Russian-speakers which are characterised as possibly leading to more communication take place in the public spaces of London:

Alina: You'll never spot a Russian-speaker in Russia [like you do it here], and it will never become a reason for starting the conversation with him. [...] The fact that both of you already speak Russian, in a way, supports you here. And no one will ever be surprised that you are getting at him. You can meet some random Russian-speaking person in a park, and make him your friend...

Alina here points to the importance of London as a certain locality that by itself may prompt or at least ease communication among compatriots united by commonalities of migrant status. The same individuals would have perceived each other as strangers and would not have had the slightest intention of approaching each other in a park back in their home countries. However, the fact that both of the individuals are Russian (-speaking) migrants in London seems to provide enough incentives for starting a chat. In other words, their presumed commonalities of identity embodied in their shared language, history and culture, in addition to their potentially marginalised position in London, are sufficient reasons for minimal initial sociality.

Expanding networks

The actual process of meeting compatriots, especially when it comes to meeting a group of them, often occurs with someone's help and guidance: when asked how they met their companions, migrants normally recall 'being introduced to each other by a friend'. Usually, the contact between Russian-speaking migrants is initiated or facilitated by a third party—another Russian-speaker, a common acquaintance. That is how, for example, a social network was formed around a bar[11] owned by a Russian and run by mostly Russian-speaking staff. The group included bartenders and their

---

11 Since fieldwork was conducted there in 2009, the place underwent changes, and the observations hold true for that period.
    The name of the bar is omitted to preserve anonymity. It is worth mentioning that the establishment is located in a central area of London, and is a common

friends—regular customers. A new person coming to the bar usually knew someone from the group who served as his guide and introduced him to the others. This social network serves as a conductor for new members of the community:

> *Nadya:* Nastya is relatively new in this company. She was working in Gaucho, and there she got acquainted with another Russian waitress, Sonya, who knew Vika [who worked in the bar for 2 years]. So, Sonya invited Nastya to a party at Vika's home. That's how Nastya came to us [later, Nastya started working in the bar, too].

The person who does the introductions often plays an important role in migrant personal networks, as they note establishing these networks in their stories. Vladimir, 40, an IT specialist, recalls getting in touch with a Russian scientist over the internet even before actually moving to London. The latter met him soon after his arrival, introduced him to his own friends and colleagues, and helped the proliferation of Vladimir's social network:

> *Vladimir:* Literally in my first weekend here, I found myself in Hampstead Heath, in a park, in Russian company, drinking some wine...I was very warmly embraced.

In some cases, help in obtaining Russian-speaking companions is provided across borders:

> *Firuza:* Inga is my Latvian friend from Hungary... [...] when I moved to London, Inga was worrying about me being here alone...and she facilitated my acquaintance with many of her London friends. Thus, for example, I met Christina, who is my close friend now, we go to tango classes together.

In fact, for many of the respondents meeting Russian-speakers in London proceeded from already existing social ties, often linked to

---

drinking spot for tourists and passers-by. It has a neutral decor without stereotypically ethnicised elements.

their place of origin. Expanding their social networks may be an uneven process: clearly, not all meetings result in friendships or regular contacts, and not all encounters are equally valued. In other words, being a part of a Russian-speaking network does not seem to be a universal aim for migrants. However, there seems to be a special role assigned to London with regard to the different ways of meeting compatriots. London may prompt acquaintances that would not have happened in similar circumstances back in home countries. Here, similarities or commonalities of origin, language and cultural background as well as the possible feeling of marginalisation as a migrant are among the reasons that motivate people to approach each other. This is consistent with the above discussion where friendship was presented as a way of protecting oneself from external threats (Shlapentokh 1984: 218). Rabikowska (2010: 291) underlines that a certain 'complex of (in)equality' among migrants can increase their need to be recognised as a unified group, and national identities may offer 'a desired degree of coherence to be countered against the host culture'. At the same time, London is reflexively recognised as a place with an abundance of post-Soviet migrants. This, in turn, makes people free to decide whether they need or want the company of compatriots; and can therefore selectively construct their social networks, knowing who and where Russian-speakers are and either contact them or just pass them by.

Above all, there are relationships with friends from home countries that are significant, sustained across borders and attentively maintained by migrant subjects. Long-term friendships are a part of almost any migrant's present social network. Quite often, such relationships are inseparable from a person's mobility patterns, and active despite time and distance. The final part of this chapter will focus on such transnational origins of friendships, exploring their persistence in contrast to more superficial 'local' encounters.

Transnational friendships?

Transnational friendships have been described as common and influential for contemporary 'middling' migrants in particular, considering that such friendships are dynamic and spatially dispersed in character, as well as the significance of its 'sustaining and inspirational aspects' stressed by Conradson and Latham (2005: 301). In descriptions of the constitution and dynamics of Russian-speaking migrants' social networks, relationships with old friends from back home are often the first to be mentioned. If many of these people seem to be contemporary 'middling' migrants, it is important to address the extent to which their social networks can be designated as transnational.

Quite often, the value of friendship is compared by migrants with that of kinship. While transnationalism studies, as mentioned earlier, tend to concentrate on the latter, the empirical observations noted here support the argument that friendship ties are no less meaningful in transnational discourse. Friendship is presented here as a similarly important variety of social bond, and this study suggests that its significance does not decline or fade away when people move. It can remain supportive despite the distance between the individuals involved, and can be especially valued in the circumstances of uncertainty produced by migration. As with kinship, such friendships are remarkable in their persistence, which is based upon trust that has been developed over a number of years. Vera speaks about a long-term relationship between herself and her husband, and another mixed couple:

> *Vera:* Oleg is Russian and Becky is from somewhere local. We met them in Moscow in 1996, my husband worked together with them. Then we moved here, and they moved later. Since November, we've seen them three or four times on kids' birthdays and Christmases. My husband is the godfather of their children, and she is Sasha's godmother. We are almost relatives! We do not meet so often, because they live in a place in one hour and a half drive from London.

> We have a meal together, with wine usually, and sometimes go to the church, as we are each others' kids' godparents...

Generally, equating friendship and kinship implies a high level of interpersonal trust is central to close relationships. Shlapentokh (1984: 222, 226) argues that friends for Soviet people at some point may start to compete with relatives as objects of close relationships. However, the contrast between kinship and friendship lies in the individually selective, non-binding character of the latter and its reliance on mutual sympathy (Bunnell *et al.* 2012; Kon 1987). Karim, 22, sees Russian-speaking friends as a kind of replacement for family support, which he suggests is especially important for young migrants like him:

> Karim: 'We are creating a kind of our own small family...[...] and I am actively working on keeping this family of mine. If I meet a good person and after a while understand that I can trust him—I will try to keep our friendship.

So, while the significance of friendship may be paralleled to that of kinship, there are important distinctions here. Bunnell *et al.* (2012: 2) note: 'while friendships may at first appear to be strongly correlated with social networks based on kin and location—class, nationality—or on embodied materialities—race, sexuality—they cannot be mapped off them; friendships are neither determined *a priori* nor reducible to such networks. Rather it is the tracing of friendships through the affective social worlds that people inhabit that reveals a new dimension to the social'. While usually transnational relations with relatives represent social connections between certain localities (i.e. London and 'home'), non-kinship-based informal relationships seem to be more flexible and do not have to be fixed to a place, and are often mobile themselves. Its mobilising force might not be so straightforward, meaning that people do not usually move to London just to join their friends (while they frequently do so to join immediate kin, or spouses); but what makes these relationships distinct is their ubiquity and flexibility. Long-term close relationships with a few people from home countries are sustained over distances, taken care of, and continue being significant when re-established in London—even if the person is quite reluctant to socialise with compatriots in general, a situation identical to Morosanu's (2013a) observations. The examples of friendships that have been 'transplanted' to London among my respondents are multiple, and are common for migrants of any social position, nationality, age, gender or legal status. Evgeniy, 43, a luxury property consultant, hardly had any really close relationships that had developed with his clients, but his few 'real friends' include people that he has known over a long period of time:

> Evgeniy: 4 years ago, a person whom I have not seen for 20 years contacted me. In 1985 he was my old university friend. He found me through friends in Germany, and we met here in London. He has become a wealthy businessman in Russia. And he liked it here so much that he decided to live here. [...] He lives in the same house with me now, I helped him to buy a flat. And he is my closest Russian-speaking person here.

An example from a different social layer is Maxim, an illegal migrant from Belarus in his mid-20s. He used to have a friend in Belarus who came to the UK and opened an office of his IT company. The business went well, but the friend was feeling bored and lonely, so he decided to bring his friends over. He invited some of them and helped those who agreed to obtain a business visa, with invitations issued by his company. That is how Maxim turned up first in Glasgow, and then moved to London. These and similar transnational friendships work across borders (but also eventually connect people in a particular location), inspire and facilitate mobility, and as far as my evidence suggests, can be a feature of migrant lives independent of their social position.

Friends often provide additional emotional support for newcomers and make the process of moving to London smoother. Alina, 28, a landscape designer who came to London in 2006, knew nothing about living in this new context. Initially, she stayed at the flat of her mother's friend's daughter Nadya, who had already been in London for a couple of years. They have continued being good friends since then. Again, relationships with immediate family members can constitute an integral social field for a friendship: both relatives and friends care about the migrant, help him/her in various ways, and worry about him/her being alone. In the case of Firuza, her sister helped her restore contact with a lost childhood friend in a similar way to how her friend helped her to find friends when she moved to London:

> Firuza: Oksana was my childhood friend. We have not seen each other for 15 years or so. And somehow my sister in Dushanbe finds her on a social website, and it turns out that she lives in Dublin. That's not London, but we see each other sometimes.

Sustaining relationships with old friends coming from the same place is rather widespread, and could be considered as a transnational practice. While kinship, as a common object of transnational studies, is usually approached as a practice of enforcing the links between life in the host country and life back home, friendship in the discussions with Russian-speaking migrants seems to be a relationship that is almost equally supportive and valuable, albeit more mobile. As well as linking localities, it can reinforce the relationship itself locally. Its border-transcending potential is often linked to the actual mobility of a person. Such friendships are usually persistent, helpful, and long-lasting. However, these relationships usually comprise a small part of the whole personal network of a migrant: 'real friendships', as they call them, are few. These may also fade away over time. In addition, while distance and time may not serve to make a relationship any less close, they do result in less frequent communication. In other words, the transnational connections between people often exist in a rather implicit way when individuals are in different countries, and can emerge or re-emerge in an actual relationship with regular face-to-face communication, mutual activities, and helping each other in matters of everyday life—but only after these connections are physically relocated to London. Relationships with someone who used to be one's friend back home are given a second life in London. Pre-migration networks, then, provide much less actual support across borders, while at the same time home-based ties, admittedly, are not easily replaced by similarly close ties after a migration has occurred (Morosanu 2013a). This is consistent with what has been said about the relationships that exist between Russian-speakers: being in London as a migrant may reinforce the need to socialise with people of the same background, but such communication can remain superficial and occasional. Since trust is one of the main criteria of friendship, this also corresponds to the image of friendship as a relationship between people who have known one another for a long time (Shlapentokh 1984: 244; Shlapentokh 1989: 176). As a result, transnational connectivity should not automatically be viewed as sustaining long-lasting relationships that firmly embed migrants into border-transcending friendship networks. It might make more sense to speak about transnational practices than transnational lives. Russian-speaking migrants' social relationships are highly diverse, and manifest various practices of socialising among compatriots and no less diverse attitudes towards such practices. New friends achieved through network proliferation, the overwhelming presence of random and spontaneous acquaintances, and even a reluctance to meet with compatriots are all exhibited by Russian-speaking migrants.

Conclusions

This discussion supports the idea expressed by Kopnina (2005) that Russian-speaking migrants in London constitute a loosely connected community of small social groups. For many of them, expanding their social networks either in London or across borders is not a priority, but rather a random, casual, and spontaneous practice. New network formation is quite passive: it 'just happens'. The presence of other post-Soviet migrants is perceived and negotiated as a routine part of super-diversity, and engaging with it is flexible to different extents, often being a feature of 'lifestyle migration' (Knowles and Harper 2009) rather than a necessity or obligation. Most crucially, the configuration and development of migrants' social networks is not principally and universally centered on belonging to a national or ethnic community. In general, Russian-speaking migrants are not universally transnational: people maintain different levels of cross-border connections. While friendships can be transplanted from 'home', reconstructed and sustained—and their significance is not contested—these ties are usually few, and do not necessarily imply regular and intense communication across borders. That is to say, transnational friendships are present among Russian-speakers I interviewed, but paying attention to the details of these bonds reveals that their transnationalism in many cases is only partial. There is a variety of ways of being connected to each other, and London is a social space where these connections are negotiated, and migrants' personal networks are formed. This localised functioning of the friendship networks of Russian-speakers in the city, and limitations to the development of these ties are the focus of the next chapter.

Chapter 4
Choosing friends

In the previous chapters, I suggested that the friendship ties of Russian-speaking migrants in London should be approached as particular relationships that have the potential of influencing people's mobility, and are also flexibly negotiated as a routine part of the city's diversity. If a personal community is assumed to be the result of the negotiation of a variety of local, transnational, mobile, long-existing, and randomly established ties and connections, then there is an apparent need to explore the functioning of these social networks in migrant lives in London. In particular, this chapter will explore friendship in the context of some of the other relationships and conditions that shape migrants' social networks. There is a variety of human interrelations that can describe migrants' sociality, with friendship being one of them. In this chapter, I develop the argument that friendship among Russian-speaking migrants is a particular relationship that is negotiated and selectively relied upon in the social spaces of London. Consistent with the argument advanced in previous chapters, the discussion of friendship here addresses how it is one of a range of ways through which subjects are related to one another, and considers how friendship amongst Russian-speaking migrants is differentiated by degrees of closeness. In the concluding section, the concept of 'ethnic networking' is problematised, as it is shown to be not sophisticated enough to describe social relationships of migrants who live in conditions of super-diversity.

Degrees of closeness

In Shlapentokh's (1984: 233-236) experience of dealing with the consequences of his decision to emigrate from the Soviet Union, his friends were ready to sacrifice other values for the sake of their relationship. However, he also mentions that such universally supportive behaviour was not exhibited by those who he identified as 'acquaintances'. In fact, informal relationships in Russian language discourse may be classified as having different degrees of closeness, and being of different value to an individual. Kharkhordin and Kovaleva (2009: 48-77) suggest a classification of informal relationships that are most commonly distinguished from friendship. They introduce an 'axis of closeness', which structures the taxonomy of personal relationships. In this part of the chapter, the analysis considers two principal categories of sociality representing informal relationships—friendship and acquaintance (druzhba and znakomstvo). This differentiation is exemplary of how a great variety of social connections can be established within the social space of the city, whilst casually navigating through the Russian-speaking diversity, which is a part of the broader diversity of the city itself.

According to migrants' accounts, friendship represents a specific domain of relationships that develops on the basis of informal communication and implies emotional attachment and trust. The core element of 'real friendship' is a non-pragmatic, affective and reciprocal attitude, as described in chapter 2. 'Real friendship' is more or less clearly distinguished from other kinds of relationships. Russian-speaking migrants provide examples of long-term and persistent relationships that they can always rely upon: meet up and share some gossip, call their friends when they are sad and lonely, and discuss any other problems at any given time. This communication is not just based on common life circumstances and superficial interests. Respondents speak about the importance of those 'life values' that underlie the selectivity of their friendships:

> Karim: You won't communicate with any random person, will you? We still do choose our social networks. We meet each other, the big world brings us together, and then we are filtered, because you would rather socialise with those who are interesting for you, with whom you have common interests. Common interests like hobbies are even not so important, but common values are. Because if you

have different interests, you can argue but at the same time have a great time together. If you have different life values, the arguments will do no good.

Friendships, indeed, have to be acknowledged as significant relationships, which might involve going through difficulties together and overcoming problems in the relationship:

> *Polina:* My best [female] friend is from Latvia, and the second best friend is from Arkhangelsk, she is in Moscow now. We had such times together! We met at work, then moved in to live together. Then we had a quarrel, did not even want to hear from each other for a while. Then, life brought us all together again.

There are numerous narratives stressing that the number of real friends within a personal network is limited. Many of these narratives suggest that a migrant's 'real friends' are most likely to be Russian-speakers:

> *Aleksandr:* In the uni...the English mainly socialise with the English, and Russians—not necessarily with Russians, but with Russian-speakers. [...] Of course, everyone communicates with everyone, but such...definite friends turn out to be Russian anyway. Well, you cannot have many friends, after all. Maybe 2-3 people maximum. Not many.

> *Vanya:* Close Russian friends, Russian-speakers—3 or 4 persons. I mean, I know lots of Russians, but close friends, those with whom I often spend my time, go for a walk with them—4 or 5 maximum.

These and similar accounts suggest that ethnic and national community concerns are not entirely insignificant in the processes of migrants establishing their social networks. However, not all compatriots who meet in London can potentially become close friends. This becomes clear when people speak about the non-establishment of intimate social bonds: the actual relationship potential and personal qualities come to the fore, while language, ethnicity or nationality are presented as much less significant:

Vanya: I think there are so many different kinds of Russians here. You can be friends with some; with others you can just have a chat, a small talk. I simply think I would not be able to find common language with all of them. I like calm, modest people...

Alla: The first Russian I met here was a daughter of my mother's friend. I used to know her before in Ukraine, but we were never friends [...] I arrived on Sunday, and she said I could stay at hers, as I had nowhere to go. And she had lots of Russian-speaking friends. It was ok for a few days, but then... I don't know, maybe they were not my kind of people. You know, speaking Russian is not enough to be friends. So I moved to another place, far away from there, and since then we just call each other once or twice a year. Well, we have never been friends anyway.

Acquaintances, as these excerpts suggest, can also be people who are generally pleasant and helpful. The attitude to this helpfulness, in contrast, is what defines the difference between relationships. While talking about their friends, migrants almost never start to recite what exactly their friends have done to help them, and what they have done themselves. The mutual supportiveness is taken for granted. This is consistent with the ideas outlined in the above theoretical discussion (Boltanski 1990; Boltanski and Thévenot 1999): 'real friendships' rely upon the participants' refusal to practice 'critical capacity' in their relationships, and refrain from assuming a pragmatic, exchange-like approach. Effectively, migrants who describe relations with acquaintances, primarily refer to the matters of help and small services in everyday matters:

Nadya: Seryozha is a friend of my neighbour Maxim. He is fun, a very interesting guy, with a great sense of humour. He helped me a lot when I just moved in. He transported my sofa from Ikea, assembled the wardrobe. He is a guy who can and is willing to help people.

Viktor sums up the differences between post-Soviet and Western social relations, demonstrating the importance of 'knowing the right person' in the former, mirroring Ledeneva's (1998, 2006) approach to informality and social networks as a way of achieving things in post-Soviet Russia:

> *Viktor:* It is normal. It's just that here you don't need to have an acquaintance, you see. You just pay. And at home everything is sorted out through acquaintances, don't you agree? No one will ever go anywhere without a recommendation [...] You need your child to go to the university, to a certain faculty. You don't know the person [who may help]—so you find someone who knows him. And address him through your acquaintance. I mean, you would not go to him and give him two thousand [hryvni], or how much is it now. If you come and tell him—look, man, I've got a child, here is two thousand, please, help him with the university. He would say—are you sick or what? That's it. And if you do it delicately, through your acquaintance—of course, he would say—good morning, how are you? You have such a wonderful child, you cannot even imagine! You see? And that is why everyone is fine, because everyone has acquaintances.

While this role of informal connections is considered more prevalent in post-Soviet countries, Viktor and other respondents report the reliance on networks of compatriot acquaintances in a similar way in London. Viktor regards it as a pragmatic way of survival and a normal feature of a city life:

> *Viktor:* No one can get lost in this world, because everyone has acquaintances. And they can reciprocally address you, because you should not be an egoist. Everyone is using everyone, and it is absolutely normal in a city.

The concepts of bonding and bridging ties that have been mentioned in chapter 2 (Ryan 2011; see also Ryan et al. 2007, 2008) can be regarded as pertinent to the distinction between friendship and acquaintance. In particular, there is Ryan's (2011: 707) argument for abandoning the distinction between bonding and bridging on the basis of ethnicity, and instead concentrating on 'the relationship between the actors, their relative social location, and their available and realisable resources'. Bonding is defined as involving 'close relationships based on emotional intimacy', whilst bridging 'may result in flows of information, advice or knowledge but without intimacy' (Ryan 2011: 721). Similar ideas concerning the distinction between friendship and acquaintance are manifested in the reflections of Russian-speaking migrants. Friends are a source of moral support, people who worry about you; acquaintances mostly provide 'tangible' help and help migrants' survival in London in a practical manner. This does not prevent one from the possibility of occasionally chatting with acquaintances, or having a nice time together at a party. Usually, friendship means more regular communication, and this communication involves intimacy. Many informants mention that keeping in touch with less intimate contacts occurs less frequently and often via electronic means of communication like social websites, text messages and phone calls. Another distinction is that a person cannot have many friends, whereas acquaintances can be numerous. Friendship also implies long-term relationships, which in this sample are often established in childhood or at much younger age, back in the home country. It takes a while to build a close relationship with a person and realise you can trust him or her.

It is therefore apparent that Russian-speaking migrants can frame their informal relationships in different ways. On the one hand, having Russian-speaking friends seems highly valued: in fact, the closest relationships turn out to be with compatriots who are either old friends or have proved their allegiance over time in the UK. But not all compatriots necessarily become friends: some remain valued as acquaintances, while others could be not noticed or even avoided. This suggests that what is actually valued by migrants is not the 'Russian-ness' of their companions, but the relationship itself. Belonging to the same migrant community, then, does not provide enough incentives for the formation of social networks. In the rest of this chapter, the analysis addresses the relationship between the limits and affordances of friendship, and the complex of features underlying 'Russian-ness'.

Constructing distances among Russian-speakers in the bar

The social network existing in the Russian bar where part of this research was conducted has already been discussed in chapter 2. Its members describe it as a social space where young post-Soviet migrants can communicate with friends, provide one another with emotional support, and combat feelings of loneliness and marginality. However, this network of friends is not all-encompassing. The bar owner's 19-year old son Volodya, who occasionally works in the bar and visits it for a drink is in a different position in the bar's power hierarchy, despite his being Russian and only slightly younger than the bartenders and their friends. Being the owner's son, he is probably more worried about the reputation of the bar than any other bartender, and tries to demonstrate it. Once, a customer who wants to order wine asks for advice. Volodya readily recommends him some wine, delivering a whole speech describing its qualities, giving a detailed account of its taste, pouring a little into a glass and offering it to try. Such a performance of customer service was rare for the bar. Apparently, any other Russian-speaking bartender would have avoided the hassle and confined him/herself to saying that the wine is good.

Volodya's kinship provides him with additional power resources, but also a certain amount of resentment from staff. He has British citizenship and lives in London with his parents, occupying a higher position in the social hierarchy than the other bartenders. Apart from that, in the everyday life of the bar he presents a constant threat of informing the owner about 'inappropriate' actions.

> *Ethnography excerpt, 2009:* Met Nastya and Sergey in the bar. Anatoly and Volodya are working. Someone told me previously that he had a habit of snitching to the owner on everything the staff did. If he had not been there, Anatoly would have given us drinks for free. So, they work out a strategy. Nastya and I go to the shop, buy a small bottle of brandy, Anatoly brings out 2 takeaway cardboard cups and they pour the brandy in them. Then they put a

lid on them, bring them inside and sip like tea. It's strong, so they ask for Coke and pay for it. As soon as Volodya leaves the bar for a minute, Anatoly very rapidly gives Sergey a glass of Jagermeister which looks like Coke. When the glasses are empty, they go out, pour the rest from the bottle into our glasses and return.

Anatoly depends on Volodya's kinship-based power while he's near—giving drinks for free would immediately be regarded as inappropriate action. But as soon as the surveillance disappears for a short period, Anatoly quickly gets rid of this control by doing an improper action. In this situation, Volodya's position in the power hierarchy is inverted. His Russian origin and language does not automatically integrate him into this informal Russian-speaking group, because his personality traits can directly affect the position of others; hence he cannot be trusted. He is clearly not a favourite: there are scornful jokes told behind his back. In this case, jokes serve to integrate the community of Russian-speaking bartenders further, and set a distance between them and the owner's son. Volodya, thus, is in a kind of marginal position—he is a Russian-speaking bartender, but he is excluded from the informal Russian-speaking community related to the bar.

The social processes in the bar confirm that belonging to the friendship network is not solely based on common origin and immigrant status. Russian-speaking migrants demonstrate the intersectionality of complex inequalities based on multiple categories of distinction (McDowell 2008b), which include class, gender, age, and legal status among others. These parameters often serve as mechanisms of inclusion and exclusion. In fact, mutual Russian-ness plays a double role: while being essentially attractive in a fellow Londoner and often prompting acquaintance and communication, as well as arguably providing grounds for mutual understanding in a relationship, it is not enough on its own to provide a sound basis for a friendship. Proceeding from Volodya's role in the bar, this analysis will now turn to the issue of divisiveness among post-Soviet migrants in London, and demonstrate what makes migrants' attitudes to each other selective and why they differentiate between various members of a community.

Divisions within the community

The assumption that migrant communities are not necessarily tightly bound and supportive is not new (Rabikowska 2010; Ryan et al. 2007; Wills et al. 2010; White and Ryan 2008). Levitt (2001: 13) writes about the divisiveness and hierarchical nature of social groups which constitute transnational communities, where 'longstanding patterns of privilege and access do not disappear merely because they are recreated across borders'. Wills et al. (2010: 111, 132-133) describe internal divisions existing within ethnic and national groups of low-waged migrants. Researchers of East European migrants (Morosanu 2013a; Ryan et al. 2007; Ryan 2011; White and Ryan 2008) discuss the suspiciousness and mistrust existing among migrants towards compatriots that exists alongside the support or assistance which such migrants provide for one another. Eade et al. (2006: 37) stress the ambiguity of ethnicity in this respect, 'since it can be both a resource for accessing capital, networks and information and a source of disappointment, vulnerability and social class transgression'. The horizontal ties of ethnic and national identities can be replaced by 'individually constructed vertical class divisions between migrants'. Thus, ethnicity and class conflict is presented as common.

The 'discursive hostility' towards fellow migrants described by Eade and many others is not uncommon for Russian-speakers in London. Class arguments are noticeable in these narratives, while another dimension of segregation within this population is underpinned by political and historical issues. The shared Soviet past, which affords a sense of cohesion to Russian-speaking migrants from different countries (Byford 2009a), is also a reason for social divisions, preconceptions, bigotry, mistrust, and conflict, most notably when conversation turns to the revival of imperialist stances in current Russian politics[12]. The patterns of inequality can be transplanted from home countries and develop under the influence of power hierarchies in London. In the uneven processes of making communities, class, ethnicity, and nationality issues can have profound implications that can either prevent or facilitate the establishment of friendship ties. The nature of such selective friendships 'could act as a security barrier against other migrants from their own national group, as well as those from further afield' (Wills et al. 2010: 133). Class divisions, as some of the respondents observed, are also connected with different levels of involvement in compatriots' networks. As mentioned in chapter 1, Russian nationals in particular have been described as avoiding proximity with compatriots in their approach to accommodation. Some reasons for settlement with compatriots include financial requirements, a poor command of English, or a relaxed attitude to illegality. Other researchers suggest that tight networks of compatriots may foster social disadvantage and ghettoisation (Wierzbicki 2004 cited in Ryan *et al.* 2008: 675).

> *Dima:* The labour market requires connections, that's why having local friends is essential. Also, education and language command give more opportunities. That's why immigrants of lower status gather in ghettos. Just because it provides support and safety for them. If anything happens, they cannot rely on the system, because they don't know the system, they are not part of it. Illegal migrants are an extreme example, of course, because they always need networks of compatriots. But if they can play with the system, they don't need them so much. Although it could be useful, but they don't need to try hard...All rich Russians I know in London actively

---

12 The (ongoing at the time of writing) conflict which started in 2014 with Russia's annexation of Crimea and military incursion in Ukraine is the most recent and probably most prominent political crisis, which admittedly had among its repercussions an increase of conflicts, and breaking up of social ties between the supporters of Ukraine and Russia within the post-Soviet migrant groups and beyond, 'real-life' and online, locally and transnationally. While the consequences are still unfolding, this requires a special research and is beyond the scope of the present work.

> refrain from meeting Russians...because it is partly a reason they came here—to escape from all that.

In the work of Ryan *et al.* (2008: 680), migrants who relied most on networks of co-ethnics were also the most critical of compatriots: 'far from compensating for lower levels of economic capital by producing high levels of social capital, socially disadvantaged groups may be divided, wary and distrustful as they compete for scarce resources'. This argument proved to be true for quite a few of the least privileged Russian-speaking migrants in my sample. Nastya, 28, an illegal migrant, has a personal network consisting predominantly of people from former Soviet countries. However, she often expresses her discontent with different kinds of Russian-speakers in London. Apart from being openly racist when recalling the resentment and boredom she felt while living in Bournemouth:

> *Nastya:* ...where there are only Kazakhs and these...from Tashkent...Uzbeks. It was unbearable. They are worse than the Indian people. All these 'black' Russian-speakers...

Nastya also speaks about her unwillingness to associate or be associated with others who could be interpreted as the stereotypical image of a Russian for a foreigner:

> *Nastya:* I like those who tend to assimilate more. I think it's better if you come here and try to look like the others. Well, not to look like...but not to stand out, at least! There is nothing good when everybody is pointing at you in the street—"hey, look, she's Russian!"—and Russians are fished out in the streets just like that. Really, from a distance of one kilometer. As for me, I just don't understand those people who listen to loud Russian music in their cars...I don't know, for me it's just horrible...You can determine that she's Russian by her face, by everything. It can be +5 in the street, but she is wearing a mink coat. And all those Dolce & Gabbana and Prada bags. No, I don't like such people.

This is consistent with Eade *et al.* (2006: 37), who underline the significance of ethnicity becoming ambiguous when 'through ethnic categorizing by the outsiders, individualistic migrants are being associated with people they would rather avoid contact with'. Avoiding contact in practice, however, seems to be quite easy. As simple as it is to recognise a Russian-speaking migrant (a self-entertaining practice described in chapter 3), it is also quite common just to pass by, or pretend you are not Russian. Above all, considering the stratified nature of the Russian-speaking population of London, it can be described as being divided into sub-communities that are aware of each other's existence, but often don't care much about others and have little knowledge of each other's lives. Evgeniy, a businessman, was utterly surprised when he happened to be invited to a party held by his neighbour's cleaner. He suddenly found himself in a hospitable atmosphere, with a lot of Russian and Ukrainian food, where he socialised with 'a whole stratum of Russian-speaking cleaners', many of whom turned out to have university degrees. Evgeniy recalls thoroughly enjoying the experience. Galya, 31, an interior designer, on the contrary, recalls encounters with lower class Russian-speakers that did not end on such a positive note:

> Galya: I was moving to my previous flat, and there was that guy, from Lithuania or something, transporting my things. I can't communicate with him, I can't! I just don't know what to say. I was moving, there were two guys, I found them through an ad in a Russian newspaper—removals, blah blah blah. I call them and say—guys, I need to have my stuff moved from Lambeth to this flat, it's ten minutes by car. Well, they come to my flat, look at my stuff to be transported, and say—hey, you are a *bourzhouika* [vernacular derogatory feminine derivative of bourgeois]! Ok...Then, we are going there in their van, and I say—guys, it seems I don't have enough cash. Let's stop by the cash machine, or give me your bank account numbers, I'll make a transfer. And they reply—ha, you can pay us in some other way! Can you imagine? I've never experienced that...my [Russian] girls I've met in the uni are normal people!

The distinctions between 'Us' and 'Them' can be reinforced by underlining the presumed integrity of these sub-communities rather than that of the whole population. Galya, after experiencing a rude attitude from a Russian grocery shop assistant, concludes that 'they don't like anyone'. Vasya, 28, a Russian internet blogger who works in consulting and marketing research, recalls a woman who has attended some meetings held by the readers of his blog:

> *Vasya:* There is a stratum of Russians here, who have too much money, and they hang out exclusively in a Russian community. West London, Chelsea. She was a classic image...spoke good English but felt comfortable among Russians. And she does not want to hang out with the English, I think it is generally typical for this kind of people...

In addition to class-based sub-communities, there are also those based on ethnic and national origins. The internal cohesion of post-Soviet ethnic or national groups in London is often perceived to be higher than that of the general Russian-speaking population when taken as a whole. Firuza, 34, from Tajikistan, speaks about the importance of socialising with fellow Tajik migrants in London, regular meetings, and the celebration of national and religious holidays like Nowruz. She has quite a few old friends from Tajikistan here. Firuza mentions that what brings Tajiks together might be the fact that they are actually quite a small community, and therefore need to keep together. Rustam, 23, half Tatar, also notes what he perceives to be the specific solidarity existing among 'Kazakhs and Azerbaijanis' which, while it does not prevent such peoples from socialising with other post-Soviet migrants, nevertheless reinforces the formation of 'their own circles of communication'. Speaking about himself, Rustam also acknowledges some thoughts on ethnic solidarity:

> *Rustam:* I think...Russian, Tatar, it does not matter.
>
> *Darya:* If you meet a Tatar here, do you think you will not *a priori* feel anything special?
>
> *Rustam:* No, why...Of course I will. [...] Maybe just a bit more than I would have felt to a Russian. You understand, a bit. This is just because it would have been a very interesting coincidence, and I know only

a few Tatars living here. That's why I would feel a bit more pleased, than if I met another Russian who are swarming the place, you know.

Darya: Has it ever happened to you?

Rustam: Yes, I have one very good friend, he is half Tatar too, like myself.

Rustam's remarks support the argument that ethnicity can be significant in terms of the formation of migrant communities and groups. Whilst Rustam remains open to the possibility of socialising with all Russian-speakers, the valorisation of ethnicity by migrants can also lead to the exclusive and racialised relationships that may appear in certain social networks and situations. National and ethnic sub-communities frequently look at each other with at least suspicion and at most with disdain, which is often rooted in the Soviet past, conflicts and nationalism, as well as current Russian and post-Soviet politics.

Lera: We've had many Chechens who recently appeared in our uni. I try not to mix with them. [...] Maybe they are nice, but they are a closed diaspora. [...] I used to be the president of our Russian Society, and I tried to ask them to do something for us, for an international event. I tried to persuade them to dance lezginka. They replied that they would not dance lezginka under a Russian flag, but only if we say they are from Chechnya...so, they would not act as Russians. [...] They think we don't like them initially, and treat us in a similar way, I suppose. They think that we think that they are lower class than us. So they try to resist us and prove they are better. If you ask them to do something, they are like—you don't like us, so we are not going to do anything [...] And they don't really want to study, and they live in this community, and communicate in Chechen, and do not socialise with foreigners...[...] Russians do not stick to each other that much. People from Caucasus, when they see each other, are like—oh, my brother, my dear, although I see you for the first time in my life...

The roots of divisions, as well as the conceptualisations of friendship, are often located back in the home countries' political discourses, social hierarchies and cultural practices. In London, they can be altered, reduced or reinforced. They are dependent on the mutual positioning of the subjects in local hierarchies and existing social networks, and are strongly susceptible to the effects of personal encounters.

Affective distancing

The above noted research on Polish migrants is rich in examples of negative assessments of fellow migrants' personal qualities. White and Ryan (2008: 1490) present respondents' reflections on the issue of envy among Poles: 'Complaining and jealousy are our worst features. If you are happy, why are you happy? You shouldn't be happy', 'Poles are vicious, they can't be happy with someone's happiness; they don't understand that there is strength in the group'. Wills *et al.* (2010: 111) demonstrate: 'Polish would never help each other...are jealous...would stab you in the back...would just exploit you...one Pole is the enemy of another Pole'. Finally, Rabikowska (2012) presented a paper at the BASEES conference, entitled 'A Pole is like a wolf to another Pole'. Interestingly, quite a few of my respondents, while almost lamenting the lack of cohesion among Russian-speakers, have compared themselves with those Poles who apparently seem to them to be more tightly bound as a group of co-nationals. However, Russian-speakers' narratives are often strikingly similar to those of the Poles, describing the alleged envy, maliciousness and egoism of compatriots. This is consistent with the argument for a multiplicity of human interrelations which are irreducible to 'ethnic networking' among migrants (Bunnell *et al.* 2012: 9). If friendship is an affective relationship, then there might be other and negative dimensions of affect that regulate interconnectedness among migrants, which shall be outlined in the rest of this chapter.

When asked if there were any reasons not to socialise with compatriots, migrants mostly noted the personal qualities that they would disapprove of in a person, while often generalising these qualities as a feature of 'Russian-ness'. In particular, many respondents made criticisms of Russian women. Masha, 32, housewife, Moscow-born Jewish by origin, elaborates on the reasons for her dislike of Russian women:

> Masha: I think I would have nothing to talk about with them, and we simply would not understand each other [...] My mum's friends are Russian, but they are all Soviet. It disgusts me. This parochialism...relationships between women in Russian communities are weird. [...] I realise that Russians are victims of themselves...their political judgments...of a certain situation that was in Russia and the Soviet Union—it resulted in a Soviet mentality. [...] I'd prefer to be approached directly, called names, told to go to hell—I would know where the person stands. But Russians...I see the relationships of my mum with her friends, who are so lovely, but then stab you in the back. [...] Russian women seem to be finding common ground out of misery. They feel pity for each other, like: my husband is an asshole—let me feel pity for you. And if you are fine—suddenly there's nothing to talk about. She cannot complain to you in this case, and if everything is great with you, they physically cannot hide their envy.

This is consistent with arguments emphasising the non-supportive qualities of migrant social networks. Hellermann (2006), while analysing social experiences of Eastern European women migrating alone to Portugal, notes the ambiguous role of social networks of compatriots who live abroad, and argues that they may have negative implications by means of exercising control over women's agency, thus showing the negative sides of social capital and the commodification of relationships. In a similar way, Marina, 32, from Latvia, tries to keep her distance from Russian women:

> Marina: The women I've met, honestly, they always need something from you. They always need help, they have problems with documents...I'm tired. Nobody helped me. I was here all alone, no papers, no rights, until Latvia joined the EU. You can meet Russian-speaking women here who are like prostitutes, just fucking around. I try to keep distance, I think they are dishonouring our nation. [...] I'm a talkative person. I can ask something, and then they start with questions—is your man rich, what does he do?

> Well, what's the matter? And I just say hi and don't mix with them. [...] I've got a family, I can't live like that and socialise with such girls. [...] There are not many girls...good ones—you don't see the good ones. You don't see many good things in life, generally. Those who try to stick to you, if they are desperate about it—it definitely means they need something. One of them was asking me to find her a man, to get married. She was offering me £2,000. What the heck? [...] Although I can't say they are all whores. There are good people in any nation.

Marina who positions herself as a *citoyen du monde* has never been seeking Russian company, and who is sceptical about the need to communicate with the familiar instead of engaging with other cultures:

> Marina: You know how it happens, you meet one Russian, and then you move into this area, Russian-speaking or Lithuanian or whatever else. I keep distance from such areas. I love the whole world, I just love to socialise and have a drink. [...] I've been there, I've seen all that. This is not new for me. But it is interesting when you meet new nations and people every day. Different stories and situations. I like that. [...] I'm a world citizen.

There are other respondents who consciously keep their distance from compatriots in London. Evgeniy elaborates on a whole set of reasons for not getting involved with the Russian-speaking community. Although he is a property consultant working for rich Russian clients, he admits he likes architecture more than the people with whom he is dealing, despite many of them making attempts to develop a friendly relationship with him.

> Evgeniy: Relationships with my clients stress me a lot, to be honest. They are all very rich people—200, 300 millions...[...] But you can hardly meet a person who is so successful and really polite. It stresses me out. So many of them are *zhloby* [vulgar people].

Evgeniy deliberately does not visit any Russian parties, although people invite him. To a large extent this is related to the remains of his memories of life in Russia and familiarity with its repressive potential.

> *Evgeniy:* …I still have fear. Although I see a policeman here, and I am not afraid of anyone, am I? But fear remains. Now they invite me to all these Russian parties, balls, various affairs—and I look at them and think: how do you know my address? I don't like being in the limelight. I'm not hiding myself, I'm sitting here—but I don't want to know anybody.

This chapter has warned that speaking about a 'Russian-speaking community' as 'unitary collective actors with common purposes' would certainly constitute an example of 'groupism', a tendency heavily criticised by Brubaker (2004: 8). Objective divisions and subjective assumptions naturalising certain traits of compatriots' character form a basis for distinctions among Russian-speaking migrants in London. They are not unique in this sense. In their study of Polish social networks, White and Ryan (2008: 1490) underline that 'the Polish community has grown so large that it can hardly be considered a community at all. Poland has simply spread over into Britain in all its diversity'. They conclude that enhanced mobility, growth of transnational connections, and the generally increasing speed of life in the globalised world led to the situation where 'there is not just a single "little Poland" in exile, but a multitude of little Polands, as networks rapidly spring up and constantly evolve' (White and Ryan 2008: 1498). Similarly to Poles or those other East European migrants observed by researchers, Russian-speakers usually express strong attachments to small social networks of close friends and family, and are critical of the wider community. As noted in chapter 1, the diversity and overlapping boundaries of the Russian-speaking population in terms of income, occupation, nationality, legal status, education, culture, and religion account for divisions. When migrants are significantly socially differentiated, intimate social ties among them are established selectively and carefully: it requires time and effort to acknowledge one as a 'real friend', and ethnicity as well as class can be negotiated in these processes. Here, I demonstrated that there can be a range of social relationships among migrants which do not necessarily work for the establishment of an ethnic/national community. By doing this, this analysis has emphasised the negative dimensions of ethnic social capital, networks and friendship. This discussion is particularly important because it seeks to undermine the 'prevailing view that good intentions and shared aspirations always inform gendered migration networks, while "bad" outcomes reside in the explanatory domain of external actors within migrant routes and destinations and structural inequalities within the global economy' (Bunnell et al. 2012: 14). In other words, reducing friendship to ethnic or national community cohesion deprives migrants of their agency in building their social relationships and living in a 'global city'.

Conclusions

As I have noted earlier, friendship is a one of a range of ways of being related to each other and being differentiated by degrees of closeness. Friendship has the potential of influencing people's mobility, but is also flexibly negotiated as a routine part of the city's diversity. Drawing upon this study's empirical evidence, Ryan's (2011) arguments have been developed in accordance with the reappraisal of bonding and bridging ties, with the additional distinctions between friendship and acquaintance noted in Russian studies of friendship (Kharkhordin and Kovaleva 2009), emphasising the importance of characteristics like trust, as well as the perceived affective or pragmatic qualities that migrants rely upon in their personal relationships. I argued that ethnic community is not a sophisticated enough term to describe the social relationships of migrants who live in the conditions of 'super-diversity'; even though ethnicity still can be invoked as an explanation of the patterns of networking. Indeed, the best friends of my respondents are predominantly Russian-speakers, and people often speak about the value of Russian friendship that presumably does not apply to relationships with others. 'Russian-ness', as a 'historically-specific sociocultural background' (Byford 2009a: 55), may seem to remain a part of migrants' ideas with regard to participating in certain social networks. However, rather than speaking about a Russian-speaking or post-Soviet migrant community in London, it is preferable to speak of migrants' relationships as unfolding under the influence of many complex structures. These include class, ethnic, national, gender, age, legal divisions both within the Russian-speaking population and within the wider population of London. The formation of these relationships is also based on affective components assigned to different social ties, social support and the actual positions of the participants.

Friendship has been considered here as one of the main constructive elements within migrant social groups, and the analysis has provided a more nuanced and specific discussion than that granted by the concept of 'ethnic networking' (Bunell et al. 2012: 9). There is a variety of ways of being connected to each other, and London is a social space where these connections are negotiated and migrants' personal networks are formed. The Russian-speaking migrants I interviewed belong to networks that may have transnational origins, and may reinforce the sense of an 'imagined community'—but the establishment and functioning of these are often conditioned by the specific circumstances of London's diversity, and are frequently negotiated locally. In other words, they socialise in a certain way not just because they are Russian-speakers, post-Soviet migrants, Russian or Lithuanian nationals; but also because they are a part of the population of London, with all its interconnections and differentiations. Since their relationships should not be considered primarily and solely as those between migrants, in the final chapter I concentrate on friendship in connection with cosmopolitanisation, as a development of open and inclusive attitudes in the domain of personal relationships with the different subject.

Chapter 5
Rethinking friends

As argued in chapter 1, migrants' mobility does not result in automatically discarding ethnic boundaries or national identities. However, this mobility can be connected with the development of openness and inclusiveness in how migrants communicate and build relationships across ethnic, national and linguistic boundaries. Relationships within diversity are complex and dynamic: a global city like London has been described as a place where 'the multifaceted nature of living with difference, where desire, tolerance, discomfort, and violence intermingle' (Fortier 2007: 110). Becoming more open to seemingly foreign, non-local things and people can be gradually developed through cosmopolitanisation, in the course of everyday exposure to the heterogeneity of society in an urban environment. This everyday exposure is the primary focus of this chapter. Relationships can be ethnicised and racialised, as well as denationalised and become more cosmopolitan—very often, both of these processes intertwine and result in a complex picture of a migrant's positioning of self within the multiculture. Friendship is one of the domains of sociality where these processes are negotiated in practice. This part of the book is focused on understanding migrant sociality as a complex of informal relationships based upon processes of inclusion and exclusion which are an essential part of migrants' positioning of self in a super-diverse city.

Becoming cosmopolitan

What is the connection between cosmopolitanism and social relationships in a contemporary multicultural city like London? Researchers approach cosmopolitanism as inherently connected with urban lifestyles and experiences (Keith 2005a; Latham 2006). Keith

(2005a: 39) outlines the levels and dimensions of the urban cosmopolitan:

> ...the sign of the cosmopolitan shelters many different shades of meaning. In its most banal articulation it speaks to the straightforward empirical diversity of routes of arrival and roots of origin of the populations of today's major cities. At another level of description it points towards a different way of seeing the city, an acknowledgement of the heterogeneity of contemporary social reality, recognition of the uncertainties of identity and the uneven inscriptions of gender, sexuality, class and faith on the social body. Yet more normatively still, the cosmopolitan, both in its Kantian origins and in some contemporary invocations, can be seen to invoke a philosophical and moral stance. Less a descriptive vocabulary than an ethical project, cosmopolitanism in some of its most recent theoretical renditions in political and cultural theory becomes a way of resolving the moral questions that arise from the attempt to reconcile different kinds of difference.

Latham (2006) outlines two strands of understanding cosmopolitanism. The first one, drawing upon Hannerz (1990, 1996), is described as the spatial and cultural promiscuity of someone feeling at home in a wider world, who has a particular disposition towards navigating the difference and cultural competence within it. Cosmopolitanism 'includes a stance toward diversity itself, toward the coexistence of cultures in the individual experience. It is an orientation, a willingness to engage with the Other' (Hannerz 1990: 239). At the same time, a cosmopolitan is not tied to any particular culture or territory, and is able to embrace an alien culture without being committed to it (Hannerz 1990: 240). This understanding is linked with the increasing interconnectedness of cultures and transnational networks which serve as bridges to other cultures. While describing a cosmopolitan culture, Hannerz points to a mindset that represents a specific 'intellectual and aesthetic stance of openness toward divergent cultural experiences, a search for contrasts rather than uniformity' (Hannerz 1990: 239). He draws a parallel between cosmopolitanism and the culture of intellectuals, and specifies that certain types of people have more chances of becoming cosmopolitan and more involved into transnational cultures. It points to the idea that the development of cosmopolitan sociability is not a universal trend, but rather an opportunity open to select social groups, who will most likely recognise the difference and diversity around them, and who have a particularly reflexive mindset which allows them to do so.

While Hannerz portrays cosmopolitanism as 'a very personal character trait', that is, he sees it as the specific intellectual mode of those possessing decontextualised knowledge and critical cultural competence, in Beck's account cosmopolitanism is considered in the context of metropolitan experience and nation-states. This second understanding of cosmopolitanism, Latham (2006: 94) observes, involves feeling at home in the world, and manifesting openness towards the diversity of the immediate world which the cosmopolitan inhabits. If, for Hannerz, it is a mindset directed towards the wider world, whereby the subject embraces alien cultures but all the while knows the location of the exit (Hannerz 1990: 240), then for Beck it is more mundane, and is an all-encompassing and universal process active in the everyday moral life-worlds of people. The cosmopolitan outlook for Beck (2006: 2) is 'an everyday, historically alert, reflexive awareness of ambivalences in a milieu of blurring differentiations and cultural contradictions. It reveals [...] the possibility of shaping one's life and social relations under conditions of cultural mixture. It is simultaneously a skeptical, disillusioned, self-critical outlook'. The central defining characteristic of a cosmopolitan perspective is the 'dialogic imagination'—the clash of cultures and rationalities within one's own life, the 'internalised other'. Beck contrasts the cosmopolitan perspective to the national perspective, which he describes as a monologic imagination that excludes the otherness of the 'other'. On the contrary, the cosmopolitan perspective is the imagination of alternative ways of life and rationalities, which includes the otherness of the 'other', when differences are accepted for what they are.

In addition to his obvious debt to Mikhail Bakhtin's reception in the West, Beck's take on cosmopolitanism stems from ideas of global interdependence as an already existing relationship that has reinforced the mutual connectedness of people all over the world. While mentioning that cosmopolitanism often is a conscious and voluntary choice for the elite, he also discusses the concept of cosmopolitanisation as what he terms a more 'real' phenomenon that is connected with international economic and political factors: the 'latent cosmopolitanism, unconscious cosmopolitanism, passive cosmopolitanism which shapes reality as side effects of global trade or global threats...' (Beck 2006: 19). Cosmopolitanisation is a multidimensional process 'whereby ever more aspects of individuals' and organisations' everyday lives are defined by their connection with things that are not local to it' (Beck 1990 cited in Latham, 2006: 96). Latham (2006: 97) writes about becoming cosmopolitan as a process of cultural globalisation, in a context of the 'internal reorganisation of social life engendered through the reality of greater diversity'. Becoming cosmopolitan accordingly means 'to try and think about the ways that a particular urban landscape, and a particular group of people, have become seemingly more diverse, more international, more worldly' (Latham 2006: 92). This process is described as internal globalisation, and comprises 'the increase in diverse transnational forms of life' (Beck 2006: 9). Beck also notes the increase in plural attachments that transcend the boundaries of countries and nationalities that make the dichotomy 'foreigner-native' less applicable to everyday life. For Favell (2008: 95), cosmopolitanism is the cultural part of the process of denationalisation, which includes 'opting out of a national system and national identity'. Despite this, national identities and consciousness remain significant and 'banal cosmopolitanism' is unfolding against the background of nation-states, being manifested in 'concrete, everyday ways by the fact that differentiations between us and them are becoming confused, both at the national and international level' (Beck

2006: 10). At the same time, exposure to cosmopolitanisation does not automatically produce cosmopolitans: 'living between borders or in a diaspora is not an automatic guarantee of openness to the world' (Beck 2006: 89). Favell (2008: xii) notes that impressions of seemingly cosmopolitan cities may fade and turn into unease and practical difficulties that migrants encounter when they face the social consequences of their mobility.

This chapter will focus on the practical processes of developing cosmopolitanism through an actual positive relationship with someone who is regarded as different to the migrant subject. Glick Schiller et al. (2011: 400) focus on cosmopolitan sociability defined as 'consisting of forms of competence and communication skills that are based on the human capacity to create social relations of inclusiveness and openness to the world', and 'an ability to find aspects of the shared human experience including aspirations for a better world within or despite what would seem to be divides of culture and belief'. This kind of sociability signifies a personal involvement in communication with the 'other' where differences between people are acknowledged but not stigmatised. The development of positive ways of living with difference has been extensively discussed in literature (Amin 2002, 2006, 2010; Keith 2005a, 2005b, 2011; Fortier, 2007). Often, these reflections are framed within urban space: Amin (2006: 1012) explores the possibilities of a 'good city imagined as an ever-widening habit of solidarity built around different dimensions of the urban common weal [...] The result is the city that learns to live with, perhaps even value, difference, publicise the commons, and crowd out the violence of an urbanism of exclusionary and privatised interest'. The everyday negotiations of difference are place-specific and situated, 'weaving in emotions and precognitive reflexes formed in bodily, material and virtual encounter' (Amin 2010: 1). In this sense, while remaining wary that everyday encounters may not necessarily lead to positive social transformation, and that people's declared values and actual practices may be contradictory (see Valentine 2008), this chapter is consistent with recent migration research which has approached ways in which East European migrants develop mundane, non-utilitarian, and dynamic cosmopolitanisms (Datta 2009; Morosanu 2013b).

Everyday diversity

When asked about their relationships with non-Russian-speaking migrants, many respondents admitted that experience of interaction with different people while living in London has changed their initial attitudes towards diversity for the better. Quite a few of them noted that they used to be 'more racist' and 'more homophobic' when they first arrived in the city. In a way, the transformation is related to the perception of London as a multicultural arena of everyday hybridity, where identifications based on ethnicity or nationality are losing their validity, and people lean towards postnational perceptions of selves as well as others. In these circumstances, personal qualities are presented as coming to the fore in everyday interaction.

> Marina: You know, [I like] normal people, who do not offend each other, and claim nothing. I like that, we are friends then.
>
> Darya: So, one just has to be a good person...?
>
> Marina: Yes, and that's it. Does not matter if he is black, white, blue, or Japanese, or Indian.

Marina has been living in London since 1998. She has had two English-speaking partners and two children since then, and very rarely communicates with Russian-speakers. She has been involved in close personal interactions with 'otherness' for many years, and is among those respondents with the most cosmopolitan mindset. She and people like her demonstrate what Beck (2006: 10) calls banal cosmopolitanism, which is 'manifested in concrete, everyday ways by the fact that differentiations between us and them are becoming confused, both at the national and international level'. The significance of personal contact is commonly underlined as a means for developing positive attitudes and relationships. Knowles and Harper (2009: 240) note that 'in a world on the move fitting in and forming connection across multiple planes of difference are indispensable skills'. Following Allport's contact hypothesis, Philip et al. (2010) regard it as a factor shaping the attitudes of one ethnic minority in the USA to another: 'as knowledge about another group moves from the unknown to the familiar and interpersonal, individual attitudes towards that group will become more positive and accepting' (Allport 1954 cited in Philip et al. 2010: 657). While it has to be admitted that not all contact necessarily results in positive attitudes due to the existence of sociospatial inequalities (see Valentine 2008), the encounter nevertheless has the potential of gradually destroying stereotypes. Clayton (2008: 263), while observing inter-ethnic relations in Leicester, underlines that 'encounters beyond the boundaries of the neighbourhood have the capacity to unsettle ideas of difference established elsewhere, particularly when they are of an intensity and duration which enables other forms of solidarity and identification to be established'. Wills et al. (2010: 137) note that some of London's recent economic migrants had learned to be more tolerant of difference through living and working in London. Among the respondents of this study, those who have had a relatively long previous emigration experience of living in the UK or other countries seem to be generally more open than more recent arrivals. Rustam, a recent university graduate of mixed Russian-Tatar origin, came to London in 2007, after living in Spain since 2001 in a town which he describes as being 'like London [in terms of diversity]—it seems that there is a relatively small proportion of Spanish people living there'.

> Rustam: Since my childhood, I've been put in environments with many different cultures, and I think, I have developed this kind of tolerance. I don't look at people as representatives of a race or a state.

The contested identities and the loss of nationality's significance are one of the possible effects of living with diversity, which also provide a way of living with it. The openness generated by enhanced personal contact with a 'different' subject essentially increases awareness and reflexivity on one's position within diversity. As I can conclude from the narratives of my informants, diversity is accommodated as a part of one's everyday life, when the subject regards hybridity, mixity, and non-fixed self-identification as mundane, an idea which is consistent with the discussion in chapter 3 of this analysis. This often involves critical reassessment of existing ideas, which Datta (2009: 360) describes as 'an inward reflexivity of [...] national history, and hence of [...] identity—one which is deeply rooted and at the same time inherently global'.

> *Tamara:* Some people have traveled a lot. A couple I know have lived in France for a long time, then moved here, and are not limited by anything [in their views]. There are people who realise the multiplicity of their own roots, for example—Russian culture, Jewish roots, let's say...

Consequently, for migrants who get used to diversity, those who seem to be different are acknowledged as equal participants of this mundaneness:

> *Zhanna:* Yes, you know, I came from Siberia, we do not have any Indians or Black people there. But I did not have any negative reaction to them [in London]. [...] I was just interested, curious—what kind of people they are, what their interests are. And then it turned out that we all are the same. There is nothing to be afraid of, they are not weird or whatever. Maybe, I am such a non-contentious person. But nothing bad has ever happened. I simply saw that people from different countries are absolutely similar. [...] Of course, we may have common moments with Russian-speakers—things that we remember from childhood. The British also do have these, they remember things from childhood, TV shows...they may like different food...But generally, there are no significant differences. Tastes, clothes style—maybe. But we all like to discuss boys, we're all the same. We watch the same movies...

While ideas re-affirming national and ethnic identities and boundaries may develop in view of social inequalities constructed on the grounds of the intersectionality of multiple social characteristics, this is not always the case. At the same time, according to my respondents, everyday life in London is characterised by an observable ethics of not paying attention, not noticing, and not exposing the national/ethnic self, as well as eventually downplaying its role as a facet of identity. The acknowledgement of diversity's presence becomes an inherent part of everyday life. Thus, London plays two contradictory roles with regard to the construction of mutual existence. It may reinforce national and ethnic identities and simultaneously cause their blurring and hybridisation. Social life in London is a fluid and dynamic combination of imagined communities and post-national identifications, as well as contrasting trends of racialisation and cosmopolitanisation which affect people to different extents in different times and places. In the rest of this chapter, I will focus on the causes and dynamics of cosmopolitanisation.

Dynamics of change

On the level of everyday life, exposure to diversity seems to have gradual and often beneficial effects on intercultural relations. Lee (2002: 81), in her study of relationships between migrant merchants and black customers in America, mentions that the more time the migrant merchants regularly interact with black customers and encounter the diversity of others in terms of ethnicity, class and personal character, the less stigmatising they become towards blacks as a group: 'as merchants come to know their customers as individuals, they soon recognise the diversity of their clientele, and this erodes the negative stereotypes of race and class. Furthermore, the process is dialectical; black customers also come to recognise that the merchants are individuals, not just racial and ethnic categories'. It can take a while to learn to deal with difference, and this process often evolves through practices of informal communication.

> Karim: When I came to Switzerland, it was difficult to get used to the new atmosphere, new social groups, I was really feeling the odd one out. But when I came to London, I was already experienced. And I initiated the contacts. Because I knew I did not want to live alone. It did not matter if they are Russian or not. If I lack Russian communication but have other—that's one thing. But if I have no communication at all and feel lost and lonely—that's completely different.

McDowell (2008a, 2008b, 2009) notes that the production of differentiations is a dynamic process where constructed differences and inequalities are prone to change and alteration. Subjects previously considered inferior can be rediscovered as people whose differences do not matter as much as they used to. It often happens when subjects change their positions from observable others to members of immediate social networks. In these cases, differences previously considered irreconcilable start to fade away.

> Yana: About blacks. Thomas [respondent's son] had a birthday, and I was thinking for a long time—to give a party or not, and finally decide to do it. I thought I would invite his friends from the kindergarten. One week before the party, I invited 6-7-8 people. But only two came. Only two black kids. It means, they are actually more open, more sociable. The white British did not come...[13]

Datta (2009: 363) describes a very similar situation in her paper on the development of working-class cosmopolitanisms among Polish builders in London: when the only kid who came to a builder's daughter's birthday was her Afro-Caribbean friend from school, this

---

13 Earlier in the interview with Yana, she expressed some thoughts about black Londoners, where she (although claiming at first that she was not prejudiced) evidently expressed prejudiced attitudes, trying to rationalise them by referring to the presumed opinion of the British ('no one likes blacks') and the views of her partner, as well as naturalising certain traits of character as 'typical' for black people. Later in the interview, she continued the polemics with herself. She was describing this situation in a surprised tone: the black kids' (or their parents) behaviour disrupted at least some of her negative preconceptions. Her narrative in general is an example of how unsettled and contested attitudes towards difference can be, and how they undergo constant reconstruction.

contributed to the development of her father's openness. It was extended under the influence of friendship. In fact, becoming cosmopolitan has a lot to do with informal relationships. The 'other' as a person becomes accommodated as an interesting interlocutor, a companion helping to fight loneliness, a person to have fun with, and a trustworthy friend. Then, such internal and personal cosmopolitanisation can be the first step to accepting a broader 'otherness':

> Alla: That's why I like it here, although it all started back in Kyiv. The Polytechnic [Institute] was very international. That's why I like different cultures. You get on well with some and not so well with others, understand some and some not. But my closest friend was Brazilian, half-Italian, half-Brazilian. At some point, you stop thinking who they are. They are just your friends, and you feel good with them.

Amin (2012: 28) stresses the significance of friendship as the key element of the politics of care in a society of strangers: 'friendship allows new intimacies to be struck and sustained, new worlds to be imagined and desired, through a relational dynamic of co-cultivation, mutual regard, and affinity between unexpected allies [...] Any venture into new alliances and allegiances—including with the stranger—requires an affective link, one that can be nourished by openness to fruitful exchange with the unknown and distant'. This is how solidarity with 'otherness' can become possible.

Social contexts of cosmopolitanisation

Social interactions in a city life that involves dealing with ethnic differences and similarities are embedded into wider social processes. As much as racialisation is often based on the intersection of different social characteristics, gradual cosmopolitanisation can also be conditioned by social factors. Amin (2002: 17) regards interethnic relationships as related to neighbourhood circumstances, linked to socioeconomic conditions, and cultural practices in a locality. He notes: 'coming to terms with difference is a matter of everyday practices and strategies of cultural contact and exchange with others different from us. For such interchange to be effective and lasting, it needs to be inculcated as a habit of practice (not just co-presence) in mixed sites of prosaic negotiation such as schools, the workplace, and other public spaces [...]' (Amin 2002: 21). Elsewhere (2012: 39) he argues that 'the micro-practices of creative forms of joint endeavour (remembering that many other forms, which deskill, divide, alienate and fuel animosity, have no such yield) have clear implications for strategies of social inclusion'. Clayton (2008: 264) suggests that power relations, cultural baggage and experiences brought into situations by its participants should be taken into consideration while assessing the possibility of intercultural dialogue. Datta (2009: 355) underlines the role of migrants' subjective locations within power hierarchies, their nationalistic sentiments, and 'the social or cultural capital that they are able to mobilise under the specific circumstances of their interaction in highly localised everyday contexts'. There are also two important points relevant to coming to terms with diversity as a gradual process conditioned by everyday interaction with diversity itself. Firstly, racialised attitudes can weaken when migrants start to interact with the 'other' in their immediate social networks and develop friendly relationships. Secondly, such communication usually takes place within a certain social group, space, or strata; which results in patterns of sociality with and within diversity that are socially and spatially conditioned:

> Zhanna: It [your attitude] depends on who you socialise with, because...at my work, for example, it's all fine. We are all international, that's why where you are from doesn't really matter. From this or that country—'oh well, ok'.

The social networks in which migrants participate seem to play an important role in shaping and modifying attitudes to difference. In addition, it is connected with spaces of communication which are sustained by state discourse, media commentary, educational practice and popular culture (Amin 2010). These factors contribute to shaping friendships with and aversions towards the 'other', as well as potential involvement in imagined communities. For Amin, there is no universal rule which would determine the development of openness and tolerance: 'other than engineering endless talk and interaction between adversaries as well as providing individuals chances to broaden their horizons, there can be no formula, since any intervention needs to work through, and is only meaningful in, the context of situated social dynamics' (Amin 2002: 14).

'Us' and 'Them': questioning the dichotomy

A superficial observer might suggest that involvement in social interactions with compatriots and with others can be inversely related. As Fortier (2007: 113) states, when problems of building cohesive communities in multicultural society arise, one of the concerns of policy-makers is that of 'outer-local attachments': 'migrants' detachment from roots is seen as a necessary condition to the process of establishing strong local ties: '"cling[ing] to some past life" [...] or ``the burden of 'back home' politics" [...] are discouraged as counterproductive to community cohesion'. Wills *et al.* (2010: 132) note with regard to migrants in Great Britain that the personal networks of compatriots often provide the social capital necessary for survival, and 'while this assisted the migrants involved, it could have the unintended consequence of reinforcing exclusion from British society'. Favell (2008: 123) mentions that migrants' inclination to avoid, or at least 'cultivate indifference' towards compatriots is a good test of cosmopolitanism. However, according to the argument that migrants' social ties are complex and dynamic, the connection between attitudes to compatriots' communities and 'others' should not be taken as a straightforward.

Strong self-identification as belonging to a national community or a high number of compatriots in a subject's immediate social networks do not seem to play a straightforward role. Philip et al. (2010: 666) underline the complexity of ingroup/outgroup attitudes, arguing that an individual's strong identification with his or her own ethnic group alone does not necessarily result in the derogation of an outgroup. Putnam (2007: 144) claims that in-group attitudes and outgroup attitudes need not be reciprocally related. In the previous chapter, I noted how recent research points towards the paradoxes of migrants relying on co-ethnics as intimate social ties, while at the same time being critical of their compatriots and differentiating between their close circle of friends, relatives and the general population of their home country or their fellow migrants (see Morosanu 2013a; Ryan et al. 2008). Such research points towards the complexity and selectivity of migrants' social connections, where close relationships can be crucial for defining a person's position within and attitudes towards diversity. Rabikowska's (2010: 294) review of works on Polish migrants in the UK underlines occasionally paradoxical critical or resentful attitudes towards both host and home cultures. In this respect, she concludes: 'migrants want to be like others and want to be different, hence the negotiation of their identities must convey contradictions'. Evidence from this research demonstrates the existence of a feeling of collective identity that empowers migrants in the context of their host culture (Datta 2009; Eade et al. 2006), while simultaneously 'their understanding of belonging or exclusion is based on individual expectations and experiences which blurs the "purity" of the collective and denies its fixedness' (Rabikowska 2010: 294).

Datta (2009), while exploring the development of cosmopolitanisms among East European construction workers in London, approaches these cosmopolitanisms as multiple and dynamic constructions for getting to terms with difference in localised spatial contexts. They are neither confined to the 'elite' version of cosmopolitanism (Beck

2002; Hannerz 1996), nor to its perception as a practical strategy of survival (Werbner 1999 cited in Datta 2009: 353). She underlines the transient and complex nature of migrants' relationships with diversity, a situation which is dependent on 'their transnational histories, nationalistic notions of gender, race, and ethnicity, and subjective positions of power that are operationalised in and through the everyday places in a global city' (Datta 2009: 367). Echoing these ideas, Morosanu (2013b) observes non-utilitarian, 'genuine forms of cosmopolitanism' that emerge among Romanian migrants who may initially lack cosmopolitan orientations. Migrants can be simultaneously distanciated from and engaged with the 'others', and this is consistent with the depiction of contemporary Europe as a crossing of transnational networks, 'a space of longings rooted in myths of origin and tradition, as it is a space of cosmopolitan identities and attachments, and hybrid geographies of cultural formation' (Amin 2012: 125). Multiple versions of cosmopolitans are produced in the specific conditions of London, where they are 'enacted under different spatial circumstances of interaction, subjective positioning, and physical proximity' (Datta 2009: 367). There can be a positive connection between close personal relationships like friendship and the dynamics of cosmopolitanism if it is understood as embedded into the processes of social interaction with 'otherness' within the localised diversity of London. The boundaries between 'Us' and 'Them' may not become entirely blurred; however, as identities and attachments shift, binary divisions may become less relevant for explaining and structuring sociality in the city.

Ambiguous images of 'otherness'

At the end of this chapter, it is worth emphasising how dynamic and intersectional the processes of racialisation and cosmopolitanisation taking place in a multicultural city are. Recent migration literature underlines the ambiguous and sometimes contradictory ways in which migrants combine rootedness and openness. Nayak notes

(2010: 2389) in his paper on the emotional politics of race that 'concepts such as "parallel lives", "social exclusion", or "community cohesion"—powerful as they are—appear to overlook the emotional connections of being and belonging and the ambiguous ways in which multicultural intimacies and visceral hatred coexist. Conflict and conviviality are performed and worked through "on-the-ground" and "in-the-moment"'. Valentine (2008: 323) writes about 'the paradoxical gap that emerges in geographies of encounter between values and practices'. These contradictions can be performed in the concrete social situation of the interview, which can implicitly and explicitly invoke the emotional experiences of encountering, living with, avoiding or socialising with the 'other'.

Evgeniy, who has an indigenous South African wife and fervently criticises his compatriots who express any chauvinistic ideas, at some point nevertheless bursts into ungrounded emotional statements about the English. Yana, the 'reasonably prejudiced'[14] (Billig et al. 1988) migrant, uses a common frame 'I am not racist, but...' and attempts to explain her attitudes with external factors like the presumably natural qualities of the racialised group and attitudes of other people. But she also apparently reports a change in her attitude, when she discovers, via encounter, that people from the group she was prejudiced about can actually be good companions. The examples are numerous: the interview is a dynamic conversation, based upon people's experiences which are diverse and charged with different and sometimes contradictory emotions. This is not uncommon in research on sensitive issues like racism: people 'may be caught in the dilemma of possessing contrary ways of talking

---

14 Billig et al. refer to the attempted rationality of racist views that underscored the ambiguity of discourse, a classic example being 'I am not racist but'. 'If one of the themes of reasonable prejudice is the rejection of "prejudice", then it needs a symbol of "unreasonable prejudice" from which to distance itself. [...] In other words, the reasonable discourse of prejudice needs its unreasonable prejudiced Other' (Billig et al. 1988: 115).

about "them", drawing upon opposing themes of tolerance and prejudice, sympathy and blame, nationalism and internationalism. In this sense their discourse, and indeed their thinking, possesses a dilemmatic quality' (Billig *et al.* 1988: 117).

Conclusions

In this chapter I have discussed the possibilities for the development of open and tolerant attitudes towards ethnically and nationally different Londoners among Russian-speaking migrants, together with a brief overview of critical theory and some empirical research. These processes occur gradually, and their dynamics are usually based upon migrants' reflections on accepting difference and building equal relationships with the 'other'. I argued here that coming to terms with diversity in general, as a feature of London and a characteristic of globalised and hybridised society, often stems from individual, informal, and mundane interactions with some particular socially and spatially localised elements of this diversity. This links the conceptual frameworks of cosmopolitanism as a non-utilitarian openness and acceptance of difference and migration in a global city with an empirical focus on personal networks and the values of friendship. Migrant sociality is informed by a combination of informal relationships based upon processes of inclusion and exclusion which are an essential part of migrants' positioning of the self in a super-diverse city.

The cosmopolitan perspective, as well as the maintenance of ethic/national ties and identities, can take place simultaneously in the everyday lives of migrants in a global city. This interest in migrants as a social agency, the ways in which they construct and reconstruct relationships with others (as opposed to the focus on general attitudes towards migrants and the latter's experience of marginality and exclusion), is an important trend in recent migration literature. Glick Schiller *et al.* (2011: 400) consider both rootedness and openness as coexisting and constitutive elements of the 'creativity through which migrants build homes and sacred spaces in a new environment and within transnational networks'. The focus on migrants and their personal networks, as suggested here, is a crucial element of migration research in times of increased global mobility, the diversification of global cities' populations and the problematisation of intercultural communication.

Conclusion

Through its analysis of friendship, this book has addressed migrants' informal relationships which are established and sustained locally and transnationally, and the construction and dynamics of social ties that form part of urban sociality within the super-diversity of London. This book has drawn upon the idea that migrants are not just ethnic communities separated from the main population and confined to sociality primarily with compatriots; but also, they are not necessarily highly mobile postnational subjects incorporated into global society. The place of a migrant group in a city and the dynamics of its development have to be analysed through a range of people's informal relationships and personal networks that may be situated in different locations and play an important role in mobility patterns. Friendship is just such a situated informal relationship which is not limited by more fixed kinship or neighbourhood ties. It has the potential of inspiring and informing mobility, cannot be equated with ethnic or national bonds, and has significant affective qualities. In terms of the implications for future migration studies, it is important to emphasise the need for special attention towards the development and proliferation of migrants' personal networks, and the need to consider the dynamics of their attitudes and relationships with compatriots and other Londoners.

The Russian-speaking migrants from the former Soviet countries which this study has focused on are part of a recently emerged and developing migrant population; one which is relatively new to the UK but constitutes a recognisable share of its super-diversity (Vertovec 2007b). Their mobility increased after the break-up of the Soviet Union, particularly after some of the states joined the EU. These migrants' mobility is also conditioned by the social, economic, and cultural trends of London's development. Most of the people interviewed are relatively young 'middling' migrants; some are in lower-skilled occupations. They were chosen as an object of research as a loosely connected, diverse and differentiated population that suggests a valuable field for the consideration of the social and spatial connections of global migration. In this respect, this book is an attempt at refining and broadening migration research which is currently overwhelmed by studies on post-accession East Europeans and low-waged migrant workers. This study helps to undermine generalisations about East Europeans as being a socially and culturally homogeneous population. The decision to focus on Russian-speakers as a diverse population was made because this population is big enough but, at the same time, in no way cohesive enough to be designated as a community. This point of orientation facilitates a deeper understanding of how migrants' social networks operate in practice, taking into account the differentiation of networks in terms of their spatial organisation, their dynamism, as well as the different resources, support and values provided by informal networks.

The explanations of migrant social connectivity that invoke ethnic solidarity, national identity, cultural background, kinship bonds, neighbourhood connections, unity on the grounds of the common vulnerability of a marginalised minority population, life in an expat 'bubble', or the universal connectivity of flexible border-transcending postnational ties, did not seem sophisticated enough to grasp the intricacies of migrants' social networks and the processes that led to their establishment, sustained them or facilitated their dissolution. This book does not discard considerations of ethnic, national or sociocultural embeddedness, but has established friendship as a notion relevant for explanations of the dynamics and differences in migrants' social relationships that cannot be fully accounted for by such presumptions.

This exploration has been built upon the idea that advances in globalisation do not universally bring change to all kinds of potential migrants, but rather add to the diversification of migration with regard to inequalities resulting from structural factors and personal motivations affecting mobility, the (re-)emergence of boundaries and the maintenance of ethnic and national identities. Different migratory situations may challenge and resist the development of postnational identities and practices, and increased cross-border connectivity can support this. Whilst this study does not deny the existence and increasing number of transnational practices, the intention here has been to show a wider picture of migrants' sociality practices, where the actual variety of relationships can be quite diverse and not universally transnational. On this basis, future studies will need to pay special attention to the development and proliferation of migrants' personal networks, and consider the dynamics of their relationships with compatriots and also with the 'others', be they a non-migrant local population or other migrants.

This book has approached migrant sociality through an analysis of the actual relationships that people develop, sustain or cut off while living as migrants, locally, transnationally, with co-ethnics and 'others'. It has consistently emphasised the relational and negotiated aspects of ethnicity. Accordingly, migrant sociality can in no way be regarded as *a priori* ethnic. Research on migrant sociality in super-diverse London should take into account the possible dynamics and importance of the role that ethnicity might play for migrants; but it is equally important to concentrate on the moments when these relationships are devoid of ethnic, cultural, or linguistic underpinnings. An interest in friendship can facilitate such a discussion of migrants' sociality that is simultaneously attentive to the breadth and range of migrant experience in a super-diverse urban context, and the nuances and particularities that pervade their everyday social practice.

Social networks established after migrants arrive in a country or those which are sustained across borders can be an important source of social support and social capital. At the same time, these informal relationships are dynamic and not necessarily centred on compatriots. Besides, they are not always supportive. These considerations are necessary for understanding the diversity and complexity of migrant social connections.

Friendship networks have been shown to be a productive basis for migration research. Friendships have important affective qualities, and are manifestly not limited by bonds of kinship or neighbourhood. The focus on friendship allows the researcher to pay special attention to the development and proliferation of migrants' personal networks and consider the dynamics of their attitudes towards compatriots and 'others'. On this basis, the researcher would avoid the risk of taking for granted the perceptions of migrant community, and approach a wider set of significant relationships and networks without abandoning the concerns of transnationality or ethnicity.

Whilst friendship has been a relatively marginal topic in migration research until recently, it is now starting to be taken seriously as a productive ground for research in its own right. It has helped provide useful insights into the patterns of relationships across space and time. The focus on personal networks and friendship requires studying migrants' social networks in a detailed way while reaching beyond relations with kin and compatriots to those with other people, as they contribute to the social processes in the super-diverse city and globalised world. In the particular empirical case of post-Soviet Russian-speaking migrants in London, it has also allowed this research to explore the legacy of late Soviet friendship as being a small-scale, moral relationship based on a deeply held sense of trust. Such friendship is intentionally perceived as being free of calculations, yet it also can be subversive and involve juxtaposing oneself to other groups, and therefore potentially ambiguous as both supportive and divisive. This historical and sociocultural background of sociality can inform the lives of migrants, their relationships with each other, local and cross-border connections, and communication with compatriots and non-Russian-speaking Londoners.

Empirical analysis suggests that friendship is a one of the range of the ways of being related to each other that has the potential of influencing people's mobility, but is also flexibly negotiated as a routine part of the city's diversity. Features like trust and the perceived affective or pragmatic qualities emerge as those that migrants rely upon and that have to be considered in an analysis. Ethnicity still can be invoked as an explanation of the patterns of networking. Indeed, the best friends of my respondents are predominantly Russian-speakers, and people often speak about the value of Russian friendship that, according to them, does not apply to relationships with others. Instead of speaking about a Russian-speaking or post-Soviet migrant community in London, the relationships of migrants unfold under the influence of complex structures. These include class, ethnic, national, gender, age, and legal divisions both within the Russian-speaking population and within the wider population of London. This book has demonstrated that the formation of these relationships is also based on affective components assigned to different social ties, social support and actual positions of the participants.

London is a social space where various social connections are negotiated, and result in the formation of migrants' personal networks. This book has suggested that Russian-speaking migrants belong to networks that may have transnational origins, and may reinforce the sense of an 'imagined community'—but the establishment and functioning of such communities are often conditioned by the specific circumstances of London's diversity, which are negotiated locally.

This book has discussed cosmopolitanisation as offering the potential development of open and tolerant attitudes among Russian-speaking migrants towards ethnically and nationally different Londoners. These processes occur gradually, and their dynamics are usually based upon migrants' reflections on accepting difference and building equal relationships with the 'other'. This study has explored the idea of coming to terms with diversity that stems from individual, informal and mundane interactions with particular socially and spatially situated elements of this diversity. This links the conceptual frameworks of cosmopolitanism as a non-utilitarian openness and the acceptance of difference and migration in a global city with the empirical focus on personal networks and the values of friendship. Migrant sociality is based on a combination of informal relationships which are connected with dynamic processes of inclusion and exclusion as part of migrants' positioning of self within a super-diverse city.

Although this book's findings are centred on the study of Russian-speaking migrants, the research may have broader implications for studies of 'middling' migration, migrant social networks and relationships. This book looks at migrants from different angles and at different scales: as individuals engaging in intimate personal relationships with friends, as members of social networks bound with informal social ties with different degrees of closeness, and as dwellers of a multicultural city employing different strategies of communication and negotiating 'otherness'. Through studying friendship and other informal relationships, such research makes it possible to explore migrants as agents who are acting in urban social space, negotiating their circumstances and creatively selecting strategies of socialisation, and maintaining everyday relationships within a dynamic combination of local and transnational ties.

Appendix 1: Data on research participants

No.	Interview date	Name (pseudonym)	Age	Origin	Number of years lived in London
1	1.12.2009	Nadya	25	Russia	6
2	3.12.2009	Katya	24	Belarus	4
3	3.12.2009	Andrey	23	Latvia (Russian)	4
4	9.12.2009	Maxim	24-25	Belarus	3(?)
5	12.12.2009	Seryozha	24	Belarus	4
6	16.12.2009	Alina	28	Russia	3
7	14.01.2010	Nastya	28	Russia	4
8	18.01.2010	Vera	35	Ukraine	5
9	21.10.2010	Nina	28-29	Russia	3
10	22.01.2010	Evgeniy	43	Russia (Jewish)	12
11	24.01.2010	Viktoria	39	Ukraine	4-5
12	25.01.2010	Masha	32	Russia (Jewish)	4
13	28.01.2010	Alla	Mid-30s	Ukraine	10
14	03.03.2010	Olesya	29	Russia	15
15	17.03.2010	Dima	24	Russia	5
16	03.05.2010	Yasha	25	Russia (Jewish)	10
17	20.05.2010	Firuza	34	Tajikistan	4
18	29.05.2010	Aleksandr	23	Russia	5
19	29.05.2010	Lucya	24	Russia	5
20	04.06.2010	Marina	32	Latvia	12
21	14.06.2010	Vanya	20	Russia	4
22	14.06.2010	Karim	21	Russia (half Jordanian)	3

23	20.06.2010	Polina	26	Russia	8
24	27.06.2010	Viktor	21	Ukraine	2-3
25	29.06.2010	Na-dezhda	45	Russia	11
26	05.03.2011	Lera	25	Russia	3
27	07.03.2011	Vladimir	40	Ukraine	12
28	08.03.2011	Yana	40	Russia	8
29	14.03.2011	Galya	31	Russia	20
30	26.03.2011	Zhanna	25	Russia	3
31	29.03.2011	Rustam	24	Russia (half Tatar)	3
32	18.04.2011	Tamara	38	Russia	4
33	20.04.2011	Kolya	22	Russia	9
34	02.05.2011	Vasya	28	Russia	4
35	02.05.2011	Ksenia	28	Russia	4

Bibliography

Amin, A. (2002) 'Ethnicity and the Multicultural City: Living with Diversity' Report for the Department of Transport, Local Government and the Regions and the ESRC Cities Initiative.

Amin, A. (2006) 'The Good City', *Urban Studies*, 43(5/6): 1009–1023.

Amin, A. (2010) 'Cities and the Ethic of Care for the Stranger', Joint Joseph Rowntree Foundation/University of York Annual Lecture 2010.

Amin, A. (2012) *Land of Strangers*, Cambridge: Polity.

Anderson, B. (1992) 'Long-distance Nationalism: World Capital and the Rise of Identity Politics' *The Wertheim Lecture 1992*, Centre for Asian Studies Amsterdam.

Appadurai, A. (1996) *Modernity at Large: Cultural Dimensions of Globalization*, Minneapolis: University of Minnesota Press.

Bauböck, R. (2003) 'Towards a Political Theory of Migrant Transnationalism', *International Migration review* 37 (3): 700-723.

Beck, U. (2002) 'The Cosmopolitan Society and its Enemies' *Theory, Culture and* Society, *19(1-2):* 17-44.

Beck, U. (2006) *The Cosmopolitan Vision*, Cambridge, UK: Polity.

Billig, M., Condor, S., Edwards, D., Gane, M., Middleton, D. & Radley, A.R. (1988). *Ideological Dilemmas: A Social Psychology of Everyday Thinking*, London: Sage Publications.

Blunt, A. (2007) 'Cultural Geographies of Migration: Mobility, Transnationality and Diaspora' *Progress in Human Geography*, 31(5): 684-694.

Boltanski, L. (2012) *Love and Justice as Competences: Three Essays on the Sociology of Action*. Cambridge, Polity.

Boltanski, L., & Thévenot, L. (1999) 'The Sociology of Critical Capacity', *European Journal of Social Theory* 2(3): 359-377.

Bourdieu, P. (1998) *Practical Reason: On the Theory of Action*, Stanford, CA: Stanford University Press.

Boyd, M. (1989) 'Family and Personal Networks in International Migration: Recent Developments and New Agendas', *International Migration Review*, 23(3): 638-670.

Brubaker, R. (2004) *Ethnicity without Groups*, Cambridge, Mass.: Harvard University Press.

Brubaker, R. (2005) 'The "Diaspora" Diaspora', *Ethnic and Racial Studies* 28(1): 1-19.

Buck, N., Gordon, I., Hall, P., Harloe, M., & Kleinman, M. (2002) *Working Capital: Life and Labour in Contemporary London*, London: Routledge.

Bunnell, T., Yea, S., Peake, L., Skelton, T., & Smith, M. (2012) 'Geographies of Friendship', *Progress in Human Geography* 36(4): 490-507.

Byford, A. (2009a) '"The Last Soviet Generation" in Britain', in J. Fernandez (ed.) *Diasporas: Critical and Inter-Disciplinary Perspectives*, The Inter-Disciplinary Press. Online. Available HTTP: <http://www.inter-disciplinary.net/publishing/id-press/ebooks/diasporas/> (accessed 13 Oct 2009).

Byford, A. (2009b) '"Russian Wives": A Snapshot of the Stereotype', in *National Identity in Russia from 1961 : Traditions and Deterritorialisation*, Newsletter №3 (May 2009). Online. Available HTTP: <http://www.mod-langs.ox.ac.uk/russian/nationalism/newsletter.htm> (accessed 13 October 2009).

Calhoun, C., Rojek, C. & Turner, B. (eds.) (2005) *The Sage Handbook of Sociology*. London: Sage Publications.

Cheong, P.H., Edwards, R., Solomos, J. (2007) 'Immigration, Social Cohesion and Social Capital: A Critical Review', *Critical Social Policy*, 27(1): 24-49.

Cheshire, J. (2012) 'Mapped: Twitter Languages in London', *Spatial.ly*, 22 October. Online. Available HTTP: <http://spatialanalysis.co.uk/2012/10/londons-twitter-languages/> (accessed 30 July 2013).

Clayton, J. (2008) 'Everyday Geographies of Marginality and Encounter in the Multicultural City' in C. Dwyer, C. Bressey (eds) *New Geographies of Race and Racism*, Aldershot: Ashgate: 255-269.

Cohen, R. (2008) *Global Diasporas*, 2nd edn, London: Routledge.

Conradson, D., & Latham, A. (2005a) 'Friendship Networks and Transnationality in a World City: Antipodean Migrants in London', *Journal of Ethnic and Migration Studies* 31(2): 287-305.

Conradson, D., Latham, A. (2005b) 'Transnational Urbanism: Attending to Everyday Practices and Mobilities', *Journal of Ethnic and Migration Studies* 31(2): 227-233.

Conversi, D. (2012) 'Irresponsible Radicalisation: Diasporas, Globalisation and Long-Distance Nationalism in the Digital Age', *Journal of Ethnic and Migration Studies*, 38(9): 1357-1379.

Cornell, S.E., & Hartmann, D. (2007) *Ethnicity and Race: Making Identities in a Changing World,* Thousand Oaks, Calif, Pine Forge Press, an Imprint of Sage Publication.

Dahinden, J. (2009) 'Are we all Transnationals Now? Network Transnationalism and Transnational Subjectivity: The Differing Impacts of Globalization on the Inhabitants of a Small Swiss City', *Ethnic and Racial Studies*, 32(8): 1365-1386.

Datta, A. (2009) 'Places of Everyday Cosmopolitanisms: East European Construction Workers in London', *Environment and Planning A* 41: 353-370.

Datta, A., & Brickell, K. (2009) '"We Have a Little Bit More Finesse, as a nation": Constructing the Polish Worker in London's Building Sites', *Antipode* 41(3): 439-464.

Dmitrieva, O., & Yuferova, Y. (2011) 'Why are Russians Moving to Britain?' Roundtable discussion. Online. Available HTTP: <http://www.telegraph.co.uk/sponsored/russianow/society/8476412/Why-are-Russians-moving-to-Britain.html> (accessed 14 December 2011).

Eade, J., Drinkwater, S., & Garapich, M.P. (2006) *Class and Ethnicity—Polish Migrants in London*, Full Research Report. ESRC End of Award Report, RES-000-22-1294. Swindon: ESRC.

Eriksen, T.H. (2002) *Ethnicity and Nationalism*, London, Pluto Press.

Favell, A. (2001) 'Migration, Mobility and Globaloney: Metaphors and Rhetoric in the Sociology of Globalization', *Global Networks*, 1(4), 389-398.

Favell, A. (2003) 'Eurostars and Eurocities: Towards a Sociology of Free Moving Professionals in Western Europe'. Working Paper, Center for Comparative Immigration Studies, UC San Diego.

Favell, A. (2008) Eurostars and Eurocities: Free Movement and Mobility in an Integrating Europe, Malden, Mass.; Oxford: Blackwell.

Fenton, S. (2010). *Ethnicity*, Cambridge, UK, Polity Press.

Fischer, C. (1977) *Networks and Places: Social Relationships in the Urban Setting,* New York, Free Press.

Fortier, A-M. (2007) 'Too Close for Comfort: Loving Thy Neighbour and the Management of Multicultural Intimacies', *Environment and Planning D: Society and Space,* 25: 104-119.

Garapich, M. (2012) 'Between Cooperation and Hostility—Constructions of Ethnicity and Social Class among Polish Migrants in London' *Annales Universitatis Paedagogicae Cracoviensis. Studia Sociologica (Annales Universitatis Paedagogicae Cracoviensis. Studia Sociologica),* IV(2): 31-45.

Glick Schiller, N. & Fouron, G. (1999) Terrains of Blood and Nation: Haitian Transnational Social Fields. *Ethnic and Racial Studies*, 22(2): 340-366.

Glick Schiller, N., & Çağlar, A. (2009) 'Towards a Comparative Theory of Locality in Migration Studies: Migrant Incorporation and City Scale', *Journal of Ethnic and Migration Studies*, 35(2), 177-202.

Glick Schiller, N., Basch, L., & Szanton Blanc, C. (1995) 'From Immigrant to Transmigrant: Theorizing Transnational Migration', *Anthropological Quarterly* 68(1): 48-63.

Glick Schiller, N., Darieva, T., & Gruner-Domic, S. (2011) 'Defining Cosmopolitan Sociability in a Transnational Age. An Introduction', *Ethnic and Racial Studies*, 34(3): 399-418.

Grechaninova, M. (2007) 'Russkaya emigratsiia—obshchnost rasobshchennykh' *The BBC*, 22 January. Online. Available HTTP: <http://news.bbc.co.uk/hi/russian/uk/newsid_6283000/6283265.stm> (accessed 25 February 2009).

Gruner-Domic, S. (2011) 'Transnational Lifestyles as a New Form of Cosmopolitan Social Identification? Latin American Women in German Urban Spaces', *Ethnic and Racial Studies*, 34(3), 471-489.

Guarnizo, L. (1997) 'The Emergence of a Transnational Social Formation and The Mirage of Return Migration Among Dominican Transmigrants', *Identities: Global Studies in Culture and Power*, 4(2): 281-322.

Guarnizo, L., & Smith, M.P. (1998) 'The Locations of Transnationalism', in M.P. Smith & L. Guarnizo (eds.) *Transnationalism from Below*, New Brunswick: Transaction Publishers: 3-34.

Hall, S. (1990) 'Cultural Identity and Diaspora', in J. Rutherford (ed.) *Identity: Community, Culture, Difference*, London: Lawrence and Wishart: 222-237.

Hall, S. (2011) 'Educational Ties, Social Capital and the Translocal (re)Production of MBA alumni networks', *Global Networks* 11(1), 118–138.

Hannerz, U. (1990) 'Cosmopolitans and Locals in World Culture', *Theory, Culture and Society* 7: 237-251.

Hannerz, U. (1992) *Cultural Complexity: Studies in the Social Organization of Meaning*, New York: Columbia University Press.

Hannerz, U. (1996) *Transnational Connections: Culture, People, Places*, London and New York: Routledge.

Hellermann, C. (2006) 'Migrating Alone: Tackling Social Capital? Women from Eastern Europe in Portugal', *Ethnic and Racial Studies*, 29(6): 1135-1152.

Ho, E. (2008) 'Citizenship, Migration and Transnationalism: A Review and Critical Interventions', *Geography Compass* 2(5): 1286-1300.

International Organization for Migration (2007) *Russia: Mapping Exercise*, London, July 2007.

Jenkins, R. (2008) *Rethinking Ethnicity*, Thousand Oaks, CA, SAGE Publications.

Keith, M. (2005a) *After the Cosmopolitan? Multicultural Cities and the Future of Racism*, London; New York: Routledge.

Keith, M. (2005b) 'Racialization and the Public Spaces of the Multicultural City', in K. Murji, and J. Solomos, (eds.), *Racialization*, Oxford: Oxford University Press: 249-270.

Keith, M. (2011) 'Between Being and Becoming? Rights, Responsibilities and the Politics of Multiculture in the New East End', *Sociological Research Online*, 13(5)11, Online. Available HTTP: <http://www.socresonline.org.uk/13/5/11.html> (accessed 4 April 2012).

Kennedy, P. (2004) 'Making Global Society: Friendship Networks Among Transnational Professionals in the Building Design Industry', *Global Networks* 4(2), 157-179.

Kharkhordin, O. (1999) *The Collective and the Individual in Russia: A study of Practices*, University of California Press.

Kharkhordin, O., & Kovaleva, A. (2009) 'Gradastsii blizosti v sovremennoi rossiiskoi druzhbe', in O. Kharkhordin (ed.) *Druzhba: Ocherki po teorii praktik*, St Petersburg: European University at St Petersburg Press.

Kharkhordin, O., ed. (2009) *Druzhba: Ocherki po teorii praktik*, St Petersburg: European University at St Petersburg Press.

Knowles, C., & Harper, D. (2009) *Hong Kong: Migrant Lives, Landscapes, and Journeys*, Chicago; London: University of Chicago Press.

Kon, I. (1987) *Druzhba—etiko-psikhologicheskii ocherk*, Moscow: Politizdat.

Koopmans, R. (2004) 'Migrant Mobilisation and Political Opportunities: Variation among German Cities and a Comparison with the United Kingdom and the Netherlands', *Journal of Ethnic and Migration Studies*, 30(3): 449-470.

Kopnina, H. (2005) *East to West migration: Russian Migrants in Western Europe*, Burlington, VT: Ashgate.

Latham, A. (2006) 'Sociality and the Cosmopolitan Imagination: National, Cosmopolitan and Local Imaginaries in Auckland, New Zealand' in J. Binnie (ed.) *Cosmopolitan Urbanism*, London: Routledge: 89-112.

Ledeneva, A. (1998) *Russia's Economy of Favours*. Cambridge, UK: Cambridge University Press.

Ledeneva, A. (2006) *How Russia Really Works*. Ithaca N.Y.: Cornell University Press.

Lee, J. (2002) *Civility in the City: Blacks, Jews, and Koreans in Urban America*, Cambridge, Mass.: Harvard University Press.

Levitt, P. & Glick Schiller, N. (2004). 'Conceptualizing Simultaneity: A Transnational Social Field Perspective on Society', *International Migration Review*, 38(3): 1002-1039.

Levitt, P. (2001) *The Transnational Villagers*, Berkeley and Los Angeles: University of California Press.

Malyutina, D. (2012) 'The Beginning and End of a Beautiful Friendship: Ethical Issues in the Ethnographic Study of Sociality amongst Russian-speaking Migrants in London', in U. Ziemer, (ed.), *East European Diasporas, Migration and Cosmopolitanism*. Routledge, London: 107-122.

Malyutina, D. (2014) 'Reflections on Positionality from a Russian Woman Interviewing Russian-speaking Women in London', *Sociological Research Online* 19(4). Online. Available HTTP: <http://www.socresonline.org.uk/19/4/15.html> (accessed 1 December 2014).

McDowell, L. (2008a) 'On the Significance of Being White: European Migrant Workers in the British Economy in the 1940s and 2000s', in C. Dwyer & C. Bressey (eds.) *New Geographies of Race and Racism*, Aldershot: Ashgate: 51-67.

McDowell, L. (2008b) 'Thinking Through Work: Complex Inequalities, Constructions of Difference and Trans-national Migrants', *Progress in Human Geography* 32(4): 491–507.

McDowell, L. (2009) 'Old and New European Economic Migrants: Whiteness and Managed Migration Policies', *Journal of Ethnic and Migration Studies*, 35(1): 19-36.

Menjívar, C. (2000) *Fragmented Ties: Salvadoran Immigrant Networks in America*. Berkeley, University of California Press.

Morawska (2004) 'Exploring Diversity in Immigrant Assimilation and Transnationalism: Poles and Russian Jews in Philadelphia', *International Migration Review*, 38(4), 1372-1412.

Morgunova, O. (2009) 'Den' segodnyashnii: britanskie russkie ili russkie britantsy?' in N. Makarova & O. Morgunova (eds.) *Russkoe prisutstvie v Britanii*, M.: Sovremennaya ekonomika i pravo: 37-47.

Morgunova, O. (2012) 'National Living On-Line? Some Aspects of the Russophone e-Diaspora map', (April) *e-Diasporas Atlas*.

Morosanu, L. (2010) 'Mixed Migrant Social Ties and Social Capital in Migration Research', CARIM AS 2010/43, Robert Schuman Centre for Advanced Studies, San Domenico di Fiesole (FI): European University Institute.

Morosanu, L. (2013a) 'Between Fragmented Ties and 'Soul Friendships': The Cross-Border Social Connections of Young Romanians in London', *Journal of Ethnic and Migration Studies*, 39(3): 353-372.

Morosanu, L. (2013b) '"We all Eat the Same Bread": the Roots and Limits of Cosmopolitan Bridging ties Developed by Romanians in London', *Ethnic and Racial Studies*, 36(12): 2160-2181.

Nayak, A. (2010) 'Race, Affect, and Emotion: Young People, Racism, and Graffiti in the Postcolonial English suburbs', *Environment and Planning A*, 42: 2370-2392.

Ong, A. (1999) *Flexible Citizenship: The Cultural Logics of Transnationality*, Durham: Duke University Press.

ONS (2013a) '2011 Census: Main Language (detailed), Local Authorities in England and Wales', Online. Available HTTP: <http://www.ons.gov.uk/ons/rel/census/2011-census/key-statistics-and-quick-statistics-for-wards-and-output-areas-in-england-and-wales/rft-qs204ew.xls> (accessed 25 August 2014).

ONS (2013b) 'Population by Country of Birth and Nationality Tables, January 2012 to December 2012', Online. Available HTTP: <http://www.ons.gov.uk/ons/rel/migration1/population-by-country-of-birth-and-nationality/2012/population-by-country-of-birth-and-nationality-tables-january-2012-to-december-2012.xls> (accessed 1 April 2014).

Pahl, R. (2000) *On Friendship*, Cambridge, Polity Press.

Philip, C.L., Mahalingam, R. & Sellers, R.M. (2010) 'Understanding East Indians' Attitudes Toward African Americans: Do Mainstream Prejudicial Attitudes Transfer to Immigrants?', *Journal of Ethnic and Migration Studies*, 36(4): 651-671.

Portes, A. (2000) 'Globalization from Below: the Rise of Transnational Communities', in D. Kalb (ed.) *The Ends of Globalization: Bringing Society Back in*, Rowman & Littlefield Publishers: 253-273.

Portes, A. (2001) 'Introduction: the Debates and Significance of Immigrant Transnationalism', *Global Networks* 1(3): 181-193.

Portes, A., Guarnizo, L.E., & Haller, W.J. (2002) 'Transnational Entrepreneurs: an Alternative Form of Immigrant Economic Adaptation', *American Sociological Review*, 67(2): 278-298.

Portes, A., Guranizo, L.E., & Landolt, P. (1999) 'The Study of Transnationalism: Pitfalls and Promises of an Emergent Research Field', *Ethnic and Racial Studies*, 22(2): 217-236.

Putnam, R. (2007) '*E Pluribus Unum*: Diversity and Community in the Twenty-first Century. The 2006 Johan Skytte Prize Lecture', *Scandinavian Political Studies*, 30(2): 137-174.

Rabikowska, M. (2010) 'Negotiation of Normality and Identity among Migrants from Eastern Europe to the United Kingdom after 2004', *Social Identities: Journal for the Study of Race, Nation and Culture*, 16 (3): 285-296.

Rabikowska, M. (2012) '"A Pole Is Like a Wolf to Another Pole": Class Formation and Group Ressentiment among Eastern European Immigrants in London', paper presented at British Association of East European Studies Annual Conference, Cambridge, 31 March–2 April.

Reynolds, T. (2007) 'Friendship Networks, Social Capital and Ethnic Identity: Researching the Perspectives of Caribbean Young People in Britain', *Journal of Youth Studies*, 10(4): 383-398.

Rogers, S. (2013) 'Languages Mapped: What do People Speak Where you Live?', *The Guardian,* 30 January. Online. Available HTTP: <http://www.theguardian.com/news/datablog/interactive/2013/jan/30/languages-mapped-england-wales-census> (accessed 1 February 2013).

Ryan, L. (2011) 'Migrants' Social Networks and Weak Ties: Accessing Resources and Constructing Relationships Post-migration', *The Sociological Review* 59(4): 707-724.

Ryan, L., Sales, R., Tilki, M., & Siara, B. (2007) 'Recent Polish Migrants in London: Social Networks, Transience and Settlement', *Research Report for RES- 000-22-1552 ESRC study*, Social Policy Research Centre, Middlesex University in London.

Ryan, L., Sales, R., Tilki, M., & Siara, B. (2008) 'Social Networks, Social Support and Social Capital: The Experiences of Recent Polish Migrants in London', *Sociology* 42(4): 672-690.

Sassen, S. (2001) *The Global City: New York, London, Tokyo.* 2nd edition. New Jersey: Princeton University Press.

Schlueter, E. (2012) 'The Inter-Ethnic Friendships of Immigrants with Host-Society Members: Revisiting the Role of Ethnic Residential Segregation', *Journal of Ethnic and Migration Studies*, 38(1): 77-91.

Scott, S. (2006) 'The Social Morphology of Skilled Migration: the Case of British Middle Class in Paris' *Journal of Ethnic and Migration Studies*, 32(7): 1105-1129.

Shlapentokh, V. (1984) *Love, Marriage, and Friendship in the Soviet Union: Ideals and Practices*, New York: Praeger.

Shlapentokh, V. (1989) *Public and Private Life of the Soviet People: Changing Values in Post-Stalin Russia*, New York; Oxford: Oxford University Press.

Simmel, G. (1949) 'The Sociology of Sociability', *The American Journal of Sociology*, 55(3): 254-261.

Sklair, L. (2000) 'The Transnational Capitalist Class and the Discourse of Globalisation', *Cambridge Review of International Affairs*, 14(1): 67-85.

Sklair, L. (2002) 'Democracy and the Transnational Capitalist Class', *The Annals of the American Academy*, 581: 144-157.

Smith, M.P. (2001) *Transnational Urbanism: Locating Globalization*. Oxford: Wiley-Blackwell.

Smith, M.P. (2005) 'Transnational Urbanism Revisited', *Journal of Ethnic and Migration Studies*, 31(2): 235-244.

Soehl, T., & Waldinger, R. (2010) 'Making the Connection: Latino Immigrants and their Crossborder Ties', *Ethnic and Racial Studies*, 33(9): 1489-1510.

Soysal, Y.N. (1994) *Limits of Citizenship: Migrants and Postnational Membership in Europe*, Chicago: University of Chicago.

Tsujimoto, T. (2014) 'Affective Friendship that Constructs Globally Spanning Transnationalism: The Onward Migration of Filipino Workers from South Korea to Canada', *Mobilities*. Online. Available HTTP: <http://www.tandfonline.com/doi/abs/10.1080/17450101.2014.922362#.VPHWmy5Bljg> (accessed 4 August 2014).

Urry, J. (2000) *Sociology beyond Societies: Mobilities for the Twenty-first Century*, London: Routledge.

Valentine, G. (2008) 'Living with Difference: Reflections on Geographies of Encounter', *Progress in Human Geography*, 32(3): 323-337.

Van Bochove, M. (2012) 'Truly Transnational: The Political Practices of Middle-Class Migrants', *Journal of Ethnic and Migration Studies* 38(10): 1551-1568.

Van Bochove, M., Rusinovic, K., & Engbersen, G. (2010) 'The Multiplicity of Citizenship: Transnational and Local Practices and Identifications of Middle-class Migrants', *Global Networks* 10(3): 344–364.

Vertovec, S. (1999) 'Conceiving and Researching Transnationalism', *Ethnic and Racial Studies*, 22(2): 447-462.

Vertovec, S. (2001) 'Transnationalism and Identity', *Journal of Ethnic and Migration Studies*, 27(4): 573-582.

Vertovec, S. (2007a) 'New Complexities of Cohesion in Britain: Super-diversity, Transnationalism and Civil-integration', *Commission on Integration and Cohesion*.

Vertovec, S. (2007b) 'Super-diversity and its Implications', *Ethnic and Racial Studies*, 30 (6): 1024-1054.

Vertovec, S. (2010) 'Towards Post-multiculturalism? Changing Communities, Conditions and Contexts of Diversity', *International Social Science Journal*, 61(199): 83-95.

Walsh, K. (2009) 'Geographies of the Heart in Transnational Spaces: Love and the Intimate Lives of British Migrants in Dubai', *Mobilities*, 4(3): 427-445.

Waters, J. (2007) 'Roundabout Routes and Sanctuary Schools': the Role of Situated Educational Practices and Habitus in the Creation of Transnational Professionals' *Global Networks*, 7(4): 477-497.

Wellman, B. (1979) 'The Community Question: The Intimate Networks of East Yorkers', *American Journal of Sociology* 84: 1201-1231.

Wellman, B., & Frank, K. (2001) 'Network Capital in a Multi-Level World: Getting Support from Personal Communities', in N. Lin, K. Cook, and R. Burt (eds.) *Social Capital: Theory and Research*, Chicago, Aldine DeGruyter: 233-273.

Wellman, B., & Wortley, S. (1990) 'Different Strokes from Different Folks: Community Ties and Social Support', *American Journal of Sociology* 96: 558-88.

Wellman, B., Carrington, P.J., & Hall, A. (1988) 'Networks as Personal Communities', in B. Wellman and S. D. Berkowitz (eds.) *Social Structures: A Network Analysis*, Cambridge, Cambridge University Press: 130-184.

White, A., Ryan, L. (2008) 'Polish "Temporary" Migration: The Formation and Significance of Social Networks', *Europe-Asia Studies*, 60(9): 1467-1502.

Wills, J., Datta, K., Evans, Y., Herbert, J., May, J., & McIlwaine, C. (2010) *Global cities at Work: New Migrant Divisions of Labour*, London: Pluto Press.

Wimmer, A., & Glick Schiller, N. (2003) 'Methodological Nationalism, the Social Sciences, and the Study of Migration: an Essay in Historical Epistemology', *International Migration Review*, 37(3): 576-610.

Young, J. (2009) *Sergei Dovlatov and his Narrative Masks,* Evanston, Ill.: Northwestern University Press.

SOVIET AND POST-SOVIET POLITICS AND SOCIETY

Edited by Dr. Andreas Umland

ISSN 1614-3515

1 Андреас Умланд (ред.)
   Воплощение Европейской
   конвенции по правам человека в
   России
   Философские, юридические и
   эмпирические исследования
   ISBN 3-89821-387-0

2 Christian Wipperfürth
   Russland – ein vertrauenswürdiger
   Partner?
   Grundlagen, Hintergründe und Praxis
   gegenwärtiger russischer Außenpolitik
   Mit einem Vorwort von Heinz Timmermann
   ISBN 3-89821-401-X

3 Manja Hussner
   Die Übernahme internationalen Rechts
   in die russische und deutsche
   Rechtsordnung
   Eine vergleichende Analyse zur
   Völkerrechtsfreundlichkeit der Verfassungen
   der Russländischen Föderation und der
   Bundesrepublik Deutschland
   Mit einem Vorwort von Rainer Arnold
   ISBN 3-89821-438-9

4 Matthew Tejada
   Bulgaria's Democratic Consolidation
   and the Kozloduy Nuclear Power Plant
   (KNPP)
   The Unattainability of Closure
   With a foreword by Richard J. Crampton
   ISBN 3-89821-439-7

5 Марк Григорьевич Меерович
   Квадратные метры, определяющие
   сознание
   Государственная жилищная политика в
   СССР. 1921 – 1941 гг
   ISBN 3-89821-474-5

6 Andrei P. Tsygankov, Pavel
   A.Tsygankov (Eds.)
   New Directions in Russian
   International Studies
   ISBN 3-89821-422-2

7 Марк Григорьевич Меерович
   Как власть народ к труду приучала
   Жилище в СССР – средство управления
   людьми. 1917 – 1941 гг.
   С предисловием Елены Осокиной
   ISBN 3-89821-495-8

8 David J. Galbreath
   Nation-Building and Minority Politics
   in Post-Socialist States
   Interests, Influence and Identities in Estonia
   and Latvia
   With a foreword by David J. Smith
   ISBN 3-89821-467-2

9 Алексей Юрьевич Безугольный
   Народы Кавказа в Вооруженных
   силах СССР в годы Великой
   Отечественной войны 1941-1945 гг.
   С предисловием Николая Бугая
   ISBN 3-89821-475-3

10 Вячеслав Лихачев и Владимир
   Прибыловский (ред.)
   Русское Национальное Единство,
   1990-2000. В 2-х томах
   ISBN 3-89821-523-7

11 Николай Бугай (ред.)
   Народы стран Балтии в условиях
   сталинизма (1940-е – 1950-е годы)
   Документированная история
   ISBN 3-89821-525-3

12 Ingmar Bredies (Hrsg.)
   Zur Anatomie der Orange Revolution
   in der Ukraine
   Wechsel des Elitenregimes oder Triumph des
   Parlamentarismus?
   ISBN 3-89821-524-5

13 Anastasia V. Mitrofanova
   The Politicization of Russian
   Orthodoxy
   Actors and Ideas
   With a foreword by William C. Gay
   ISBN 3-89821-481-8

14 Nathan D. Larson
Alexander Solzhenitsyn and the
Russo-Jewish Question
ISBN 3-89821-483-4

15 Guido Houben
Kulturpolitik und Ethnizität
Staatliche Kunstförderung im Russland der
neunziger Jahre
Mit einem Vorwort von Gert Weisskirchen
ISBN 3-89821-542-3

16 Leonid Luks
Der russische „Sonderweg"?
Aufsätze zur neuesten Geschichte Russlands
im europäischen Kontext
ISBN 3-89821-496-6

17 Евгений Мороз
История «Мёртвой воды» – от
страшной сказки к большой
политике
Политическое неоязычество в
постсоветской России
ISBN 3-89821-551-2

18 Александр Верховский и Галина
Кожевникова (ред.)
Этническая и религиозная
интолерантность в российских СМИ
Результаты мониторинга 2001-2004 гг.
ISBN 3-89821-569-5

19 Christian Ganzer
Sowjetisches Erbe und ukrainische
Nation
Das Museum der Geschichte des Zaporoger
Kosakentums auf der Insel Chortycja
Mit einem Vorwort von Frank Golczewski
ISBN 3-89821-504-0

20 Эльза-Баир Гучинова
Помнить нельзя забыть
Антропология депортационной травмы
калмыков
С предисловием Кэролайн Хамфри
ISBN 3-89821-506-7

21 Юлия Лидерман
Мотивы «проверки» и «испытания»
в постсоветской культуре
Советское прошлое в российском
кинематографе 1990-х годов
С предисловием Евгения Марголита
ISBN 3-89821-511-3

22 Tanya Lokshina, Ray Thomas, Mary
Mayer (Eds.)
The Imposition of a Fake Political
Settlement in the Northern Caucasus
The 2003 Chechen Presidential Election
ISBN 3-89821-436-2

23 Timothy McCajor Hall, Rosie Read
(Eds.)
Changes in the Heart of Europe
Recent Ethnographies of Czechs, Slovaks,
Roma, and Sorbs
With an afterword by Zdeněk Salzmann
ISBN 3-89821-606-3

24 Christian Autengruber
Die politischen Parteien in Bulgarien
und Rumänien
Eine vergleichende Analyse seit Beginn der
90er Jahre
Mit einem Vorwort von Dorothée de Nève
ISBN 3-89821-476-1

25 Annette Freyberg-Inan with Radu
Cristescu
The Ghosts in Our Classrooms, or:
John Dewey Meets Ceaușescu
The Promise and the Failures of Civic
Education in Romania
ISBN 3-89821-416-8

26 John B. Dunlop
The 2002 Dubrovka and 2004 Beslan
Hostage Crises
A Critique of Russian Counter-Terrorism
With a foreword by Donald N. Jensen
ISBN 3-89821-608-X

27 Peter Koller
Das touristische Potenzial von
Kam''janec'–Podil's'kyj
Eine fremdenverkehrsgeographische
Untersuchung der Zukunftsperspektiven und
Maßnahmenplanung zur
Destinationsentwicklung des „ukrainischen
Rothenburg"
Mit einem Vorwort von Kristiane Klemm
ISBN 3-89821-640-3

28 Françoise Daucé, Elisabeth Sieca-
Kozlowski (Eds.)
Dedovshchina in the Post-Soviet
Military
Hazing of Russian Army Conscripts in a
Comparative Perspective
With a foreword by Dale Herspring
ISBN 3-89821-616-0

29 Florian Strasser
    Zivilgesellschaftliche Einflüsse auf die
    Orange Revolution
    Die gewaltlose Massenbewegung und die
    ukrainische Wahlkrise 2004
    Mit einem Vorwort von Egbert Jahn
    ISBN 3-89821-648-9

30 Rebecca S. Katz
    The Georgian Regime Crisis of 2003-2004
    A Case Study in Post-Soviet Media
    Representation of Politics, Crime and
    Corruption
    ISBN 3-89821-413-3

31 Vladimir Kantor
    Willkür oder Freiheit
    Beiträge zur russischen Geschichtsphilosophie
    Ediert von Dagmar Herrmann sowie mit
    einem Vorwort versehen von Leonid Luks
    ISBN 3-89821-589-X

32 Laura A. Victoir
    The Russian Land Estate Today
    A Case Study of Cultural Politics in Post-Soviet Russia
    With a foreword by Priscilla Roosevelt
    ISBN 3-89821-426-5

33 Ivan Katchanovski
    Cleft Countries
    Regional Political Divisions and Cultures in
    Post Soviet Ukraine and Moldova
    With a foreword by Francis Fukuyama
    ISBN 3-89821-558-X

34 Florian Mühlfried
    Postsowjetische Feiern
    Das Georgische Bankett im Wandel
    Mit einem Vorwort von Kevin Tuite
    ISBN 3-89821-601-2

35 Roger Griffin, Werner Loh, Andreas
    Umland (Eds.)
    Fascism Past and Present, West and East
    An International Debate on Concepts and
    Cases in the Comparative Study of the
    Extreme Right
    With an afterword by Walter Laqueur
    ISBN 3-89821-674-8

36 Sebastian Schlegel
    Der „Weiße Archipel"
    Sowjetische Atomstädte 1945-1991
    Mit einem Geleitwort von Thomas Bohn
    ISBN 3-89821-679-9

37 Vyacheslav Likhachev
    Political Anti-Semitism in Post-Soviet Russia
    Actors and Ideas in 1991-2003
    Edited and translated from Russian by Eugene Veklerov
    ISBN 3-89821-529-6

38 Josette Baer (Ed.)
    Preparing Liberty in Central Europe
    Political Texts from the Spring of Nations
    1848 to the Spring of Prague 1968
    With a foreword by Zdeněk V. David
    ISBN 3-89821-546-6

39 Михаил Лукьянов
    Российский консерватизм и
    реформа, 1907-1914
    С предисловием Марка Д. Стейнберга
    ISBN 3-89821-503-2

40 Nicola Melloni
    Market Without Economy
    The 1998 Russian Financial Crisis
    With a foreword by Eiji Furukawa
    ISBN 3-89821-407-9

41 Dmitrij Chmelnizki
    Die Architektur Stalins
    Bd. 1: Studien zu Ideologie und Stil
    Bd. 2: Bilddokumentation
    Mit einem Vorwort von Bruno Flierl
    ISBN 3-89821-515-6

42 Katja Yafimava
    Post-Soviet Russian-Belarussian Relationships
    The Role of Gas Transit Pipelines
    With a foreword by Jonathan P. Stern
    ISBN 3-89821-655-1

43 Boris Chavkin
    Verflechtungen der deutschen und
    russischen Zeitgeschichte
    Aufsätze und Archivfunde zu den
    Beziehungen Deutschlands und der
    Sowjetunion von 1917 bis 1991
    Ediert von Markus Edlinger sowie mit einem
    Vorwort versehen von Leonid Luks
    ISBN 3-89821-756-6

44 Anastasija Grynenko in
    Zusammenarbeit mit Claudia Dathe
    Die Terminologie des Gerichtswesens
    der Ukraine und Deutschlands im
    Vergleich
    Eine übersetzungswissenschaftliche Analyse
    juristischer Fachbegriffe im Deutschen,
    Ukrainischen und Russischen
    Mit einem Vorwort von Ulrich Hartmann
    ISBN 3-89821-691-8

45 Anton Burkov
    The Impact of the European
    Convention on Human Rights on
    Russian Law
    Legislation and Application in 1996-2006
    With a foreword by Françoise Hampson
    ISBN 978-3-89821-639-5

46 Stina Torjesen, Indra Overland (Eds.)
    International Election Observers in
    Post-Soviet Azerbaijan
    Geopolitical Pawns or Agents of Change?
    ISBN 978-3-89821-743-9

47 Taras Kuzio
    Ukraine – Crimea – Russia
    Triangle of Conflict
    ISBN 978-3-89821-761-3

48 Claudia Šabić
    "Ich erinnere mich nicht, aber L'viv!"
    Zur Funktion kultureller Faktoren für die
    Institutionalisierung und Entwicklung einer
    ukrainischen Region
    Mit einem Vorwort von Melanie Tatur
    ISBN 978-3-89821-752-1

49 Marlies Bilz
    Tatarstan in der Transformation
    Nationaler Diskurs und Politische Praxis
    1988-1994
    Mit einem Vorwort von Frank Golczewski
    ISBN 978-3-89821-722-4

50 Марлен Ларюэль (ред.)
    Современные интерпретации
    русского национализма
    ISBN 978-3-89821-795-8

51 Sonja Schüler
    Die ethnische Dimension der Armut
    Roma im postsozialistischen Rumänien
    Mit einem Vorwort von Anton Sterbling
    ISBN 978-3-89821-776-7

52 Галина Кожевникова
    Радикальный национализм в России
    и противодействие ему
    Сборник докладов Центра «Сова» за 2004-
    2007 гг.
    С предисловием Александра Верховского
    ISBN 978-3-89821-721-7

53 Галина Кожевникова и Владимир
    Прибыловский
    Российская власть в биографиях I
    Высшие должностные лица РФ в 2004 г.
    ISBN 978-3-89821-796-5

54 Галина Кожевникова и Владимир
    Прибыловский
    Российская власть в биографиях II
    Члены Правительства РФ в 2004 г.
    ISBN 978-3-89821-797-2

55 Галина Кожевникова и Владимир
    Прибыловский
    Российская власть в биографиях III
    Руководители федеральных служб и
    агентств РФ в 2004 г.
    ISBN 978-3-89821-798-9

56 Ileana Petroniu
    Privatisierung in
    Transformationsökonomien
    Determinanten der Restrukturierungs-
    Bereitschaft am Beispiel Polens, Rumäniens
    und der Ukraine
    Mit einem Vorwort von Rainer W. Schäfer
    ISBN 978-3-89821-790-3

57 Christian Wipperfürth
    Russland und seine GUS-Nachbarn
    Hintergründe, aktuelle Entwicklungen und
    Konflikte in einer ressourcenreichen Region
    ISBN 978-3-89821-801-6

58 Togzhan Kassenova
    From Antagonism to Partnership
    The Uneasy Path of the U.S.-Russian
    Cooperative Threat Reduction
    With a foreword by Christoph Bluth
    ISBN 978-3-89821-707-1

59 Alexander Höllwerth
    Das sakrale eurasische Imperium des
    Aleksandr Dugin
    Eine Diskursanalyse zum postsowjetischen
    russischen Rechtsextremismus
    Mit einem Vorwort von Dirk Uffelmann
    ISBN 978-3-89821-813-7

60   *Олег Рябов*
«Россия-Матушка»
Национализм, гендер и война в России XX века
С предисловием Елены Гощило
ISBN 978-3-89821-487-2

61   *Ivan Maistrenko*
Borot'bism
A Chapter in the History of the Ukrainian Revolution
With a new introduction by Chris Ford
Translated by George S. N. Luckyj with the assistance of Ivan L. Rudnytsky
ISBN 978-3-89821-697-5

62   *Maryna Romanets*
Anamorphosic Texts and Reconfigured Visions
Improvised Traditions in Contemporary Ukrainian and Irish Literature
ISBN 978-3-89821-576-3

63   *Paul D'Anieri and Taras Kuzio (Eds.)*
Aspects of the Orange Revolution I
Democratization and Elections in Post-Communist Ukraine
ISBN 978-3-89821-698-2

64   *Bohdan Harasymiw in collaboration with Oleh S. Ilnytzkyj (Eds.)*
Aspects of the Orange Revolution II
Information and Manipulation Strategies in the 2004 Ukrainian Presidential Elections
ISBN 978-3-89821-699-9

65   *Ingmar Bredies, Andreas Umland and Valentin Yakushik (Eds.)*
Aspects of the Orange Revolution III
The Context and Dynamics of the 2004 Ukrainian Presidential Elections
ISBN 978-3-89821-803-0

66   *Ingmar Bredies, Andreas Umland and Valentin Yakushik (Eds.)*
Aspects of the Orange Revolution IV
Foreign Assistance and Civic Action in the 2004 Ukrainian Presidential Elections
ISBN 978-3-89821-808-5

67   *Ingmar Bredies, Andreas Umland and Valentin Yakushik (Eds.)*
Aspects of the Orange Revolution V
Institutional Observation Reports on the 2004 Ukrainian Presidential Elections
ISBN 978-3-89821-809-2

68   *Taras Kuzio (Ed.)*
Aspects of the Orange Revolution VI
Post-Communist Democratic Revolutions in Comparative Perspective
ISBN 978-3-89821-820-7

69   *Tim Bohse*
Autoritarismus statt Selbstverwaltung
Die Transformation der kommunalen Politik in der Stadt Kaliningrad 1990-2005
Mit einem Geleitwort von Stefan Troebst
ISBN 978-3-89821-782-8

70   *David Rupp*
Die Rußländische Föderation und die russischsprachige Minderheit in Lettland
Eine Fallstudie zur Anwaltspolitik Moskaus gegenüber den russophonen Minderheiten im „Nahen Ausland" von 1991 bis 2002
Mit einem Vorwort von Helmut Wagner
ISBN 978-3-89821-778-1

71   *Taras Kuzio*
Theoretical and Comparative Perspectives on Nationalism
New Directions in Cross-Cultural and Post-Communist Studies
With a foreword by Paul Robert Magocsi
ISBN 978-3-89821-815-3

72   *Christine Teichmann*
Die Hochschultransformation im heutigen Osteuropa
Kontinuität und Wandel bei der Entwicklung des postkommunistischen Universitätswesens
Mit einem Vorwort von Oskar Anweiler
ISBN 978-3-89821-842-9

73   *Julia Kusznir*
Der politische Einfluss von Wirtschaftseliten in russischen Regionen
Eine Analyse am Beispiel der Erdöl- und Erdgasindustrie, 1992-2005
Mit einem Vorwort von Wolfgang Eichwede
ISBN 978-3-89821-821-4

74   *Alena Vysotskaya*
Russland, Belarus und die EU-Osterweiterung
Zur Minderheitenfrage und zum Problem der Freizügigkeit des Personenverkehrs
Mit einem Vorwort von Katlijn Malfliet
ISBN 978-3-89821-822-1

75 Heiko Pleines (Hrsg.)
Corporate Governance in postsozialistischen Volkswirtschaften
ISBN 978-3-89821-766-8

76 Stefan Ihrig
Wer sind die Moldawier?
Rumänismus versus Moldowanismus in Historiographie und Schulbüchern der Republik Moldova, 1991-2006
Mit einem Vorwort von Holm Sundhaussen
ISBN 978-3-89821-466-7

77 Galina Kozhevnikova in collaboration with Alexander Verkhovsky and Eugene Veklerov
Ultra-Nationalism and Hate Crimes in Contemporary Russia
The 2004-2006 Annual Reports of Moscow's SOVA Center
With a foreword by Stephen D. Shenfield
ISBN 978-3-89821-868-9

78 Florian Küchler
The Role of the European Union in Moldova's Transnistria Conflict
With a foreword by Christopher Hill
ISBN 978-3-89821-850-4

79 Bernd Rechel
The Long Way Back to Europe
Minority Protection in Bulgaria
With a foreword by Richard Crampton
ISBN 978-3-89821-863-4

80 Peter W. Rodgers
Nation, Region and History in Post-Communist Transitions
Identity Politics in Ukraine, 1991-2006
With a foreword by Vera Tolz
ISBN 978-3-89821-903-7

81 Stephanie Solywoda
The Life and Work of Semen L. Frank
A Study of Russian Religious Philosophy
With a foreword by Philip Walters
ISBN 978-3-89821-457-5

82 Vera Sokolova
Cultural Politics of Ethnicity
Discourses on Roma in Communist Czechoslovakia
ISBN 978-3-89821-864-1

83 Natalya Shevchik Ketenci
Kazakhstani Enterprises in Transition
The Role of Historical Regional Development in Kazakhstan's Post-Soviet Economic Transformation
ISBN 978-3-89821-831-3

84 Martin Malek, Anna Schor-Tschudnowskaja (Hrsg.)
Europa im Tschetschenienkrieg
Zwischen politischer Ohnmacht und Gleichgültigkeit
Mit einem Vorwort von Lipchan Basajewa
ISBN 978-3-89821-676-0

85 Stefan Meister
Das postsowjetische Universitätswesen zwischen nationalem und internationalem Wandel
Die Entwicklung der regionalen Hochschule in Russland als Gradmesser der Systemtransformation
Mit einem Vorwort von Joan DeBardeleben
ISBN 978-3-89821-891-7

86 Konstantin Sheiko in collaboration with Stephen Brown
Nationalist Imaginings of the Russian Past
Anatolii Fomenko and the Rise of Alternative History in Post-Communist Russia
With a foreword by Donald Ostrowski
ISBN 978-3-89821-915-0

87 Sabine Jenni
Wie stark ist das „Einige Russland"?
Zur Parteibindung der Eliten und zum Wahlerfolg der Machtpartei im Dezember 2007
Mit einem Vorwort von Klaus Armingeon
ISBN 978-3-89821-961-7

88 Thomas Borén
Meeting-Places of Transformation
Urban Identity, Spatial Representations and Local Politics in Post-Soviet St Petersburg
ISBN 978-3-89821-739-2

89 Aygul Ashirova
Stalinismus und Stalin-Kult in Zentralasien
Turkmenistan 1924-1953
Mit einem Vorwort von Leonid Luks
ISBN 978-3-89821-987-7

90   Leonid Luks
     Freiheit oder imperiale Größe?
     Essays zu einem russischen Dilemma
     ISBN 978-3-8382-0011-8

91   Christopher Gilley
     The 'Change of Signposts' in the
     Ukrainian Emigration
     A Contribution to the History of
     Sovietophilism in the 1920s
     With a foreword by Frank Golczewski
     ISBN 978-3-89821-965-5

92   Philipp Casula, Jeronim Perovic
     (Eds.)
     Identities and Politics
     During the Putin Presidency
     The Discursive Foundations of Russia's
     Stability
     With a foreword by Heiko Haumann
     ISBN 978-3-8382-0015-6

93   Marcel Viëtor
     Europa und die Frage
     nach seinen Grenzen im Osten
     Zur Konstruktion ‚europäischer Identität' in
     Geschichte und Gegenwart
     Mit einem Vorwort von Albrecht Lehmann
     ISBN 978-3-8382-0045-3

94   Ben Hellman, Andrei Rogachevskii
     Filming the Unfilmable
     Caspar Wrede's 'One Day in the Life
     of Ivan Denisovich'
     Second, Revised and Expanded Edition
     ISBN 978-3-8382-0044-6

95   Eva Fuchslocher
     Vaterland, Sprache, Glaube
     Orthodoxie und Nationenbildung
     am Beispiel Georgiens
     Mit einem Vorwort von Christina von Braun
     ISBN 978-3-89821-884-9

96   Vladimir Kantor
     Das Westlertum und der Weg
     Russlands
     Zur Entwicklung der russischen Literatur und
     Philosophie
     Ediert von Dagmar Herrmann
     Mit einem Beitrag von Nikolaus Lobkowicz
     ISBN 978-3-8382-0102-3

97   Kamran Musayev
     Die postsowjetische Transformation
     im Baltikum und Südkaukasus
     Eine vergleichende Untersuchung der
     politischen Entwicklung Lettlands und
     Aserbaidschans 1985-2009
     Mit einem Vorwort von Leonid Luks
     Ediert von Sandro Henschel
     ISBN 978-3-8382-0103-0

98   Tatiana Zhurzhenko
     Borderlands into Bordered Lands
     Geopolitics of Identity in Post-Soviet Ukraine
     With a foreword by Dieter Segert
     ISBN 978-3-8382-0042-2

99   Кирилл Галушко, Лидия Смола
     (ред.)
     Пределы падения – варианты
     украинского будущего
     Аналитико-прогностические исследования
     ISBN 978-3-8382-0148-1

100 Michael Minkenberg (ed.)
     Historical Legacies and the Radical
     Right in Post-Cold War Central and
     Eastern Europe
     With an afterword by Sabrina P. Ramet
     ISBN 978-3-8382-0124-5

101 David-Emil Wickström
     Rocking St. Petersburg
     Transcultural Flows and Identity Politics in
     the St. Petersburg Popular Music Scene
     With a foreword by Yngvar B. Steinholt
     Second, Revised and Expanded Edition
     ISBN 978-3-8382-0100-9

102 Eva Zabka
     Eine neue „Zeit der Wirren"?
     Der spät- und postsowjetische Systemwandel
     1985-2000 im Spiegel russischer
     gesellschaftspolitischer Diskurse
     Mit einem Vorwort von Margareta Mommsen
     ISBN 978-3-8382-0161-0

103 Ulrike Ziemer
     Ethnic Belonging, Gender and
     Cultural Practices
     Youth Identitites in Contemporary Russia
     With a foreword by Anoop Nayak
     ISBN 978-3-8382-0152-8

104 Ksenia Chepikova
‚Einiges Russland' - eine zweite KPdSU?
Aspekte der Identitätskonstruktion einer postsowjetischen „Partei der Macht"
Mit einem Vorwort von Torsten Oppelland
ISBN 978-3-8382-0311-9

105 Леонид Люкс
Западничество или евразийство? Демократия или идеократия?
Сборник статей об исторических дилеммах России
С предисловием Владимира Кантора
ISBN 978-3-8382-0211-2

106 Anna Dost
Das russische Verfassungsrecht auf dem Weg zum Föderalismus und zurück
Zum Konflikt von Rechtsnormen und -wirklichkeit in der Russländischen Föderation von 1991 bis 2009
Mit einem Vorwort von Alexander Blankenagel
ISBN 978-3-8382-0292-1

107 Philipp Herzog
Sozialistische Völkerfreundschaft, nationaler Widerstand oder harmloser Zeitvertreib?
Zur politischen Funktion der Volkskunst im sowjetischen Estland
Mit einem Vorwort von Andreas Kappeler
ISBN 978-3-8382-0216-7

108 Marlène Laruelle (ed.)
Russian Nationalism, Foreign Policy, and Identity Debates in Putin's Russia
New Ideological Patterns after the Orange Revolution
ISBN 978-3-8382-0325-6

109 Michail Logvinov
Russlands Kampf gegen den internationalen Terrorismus
Eine kritische Bestandsaufnahme des Bekämpfungsansatzes
Mit einem Geleitwort von Hans-Henning Schröder
und einem Vorwort von Eckhard Jesse
ISBN 978-3-8382-0329-4

110 John B. Dunlop
The Moscow Bombings of September 1999
Examinations of Russian Terrorist Attacks at the Onset of Vladimir Putin's Rule
Second, Revised and Expanded Edition
ISBN 978-3-8382-0388-1

111 Андрей А. Ковалёв
Свидетельство из-за кулис российской политики I
Можно ли делать добро из зла?
(Воспоминания и размышления о последних советских и первых послесоветских годах)
With a foreword by Peter Reddaway
ISBN 978-3-8382-0302-7

112 Андрей А. Ковалёв
Свидетельство из-за кулис российской политики II
Угроза для себя и окружающих
(Наблюдения и предостережения относительно происходящего после 2000 г.)
ISBN 978-3-8382-0303-4

113 Bernd Kappenberg
Zeichen setzen für Europa
Der Gebrauch europäischer lateinischer Sonderzeichen in der deutschen Öffentlichkeit
Mit einem Vorwort von Peter Schlobinski
ISBN 978-3-89821-749-1

114 Ivo Mijnssen
The Quest for an Ideal Youth in Putin's Russia I
Back to Our Future! History, Modernity, and Patriotism according to Nashi, 2005-2013
With a foreword by Jeronim Perović
Second, Revised and Expanded Edition
ISBN 978-3-8382-0368-3

115 Jussi Lassila
The Quest for an Ideal Youth in Putin's Russia II
The Search for Distinctive Conformism in the Political Communication of Nashi, 2005-2009
With a foreword by Kirill Postoutenko
Second, Revised and Expanded Edition
ISBN 978-3-8382-0415-4

116 Valerio Trabandt
Neue Nachbarn, gute Nachbarschaft?
Die EU als internationaler Akteur am Beispiel ihrer Demokratieförderung in Belarus und der Ukraine 2004-2009
Mit einem Vorwort von Jutta Joachim
ISBN 978-3-8382-0437-6

117 Fabian Pfeiffer
     Estlands Außen- und Sicherheitspolitik I
     Der estnische Atlantizismus nach der
     wiedererlangten Unabhängigkeit 1991-2004
     Mit einem Vorwort von Helmut Hubel
     ISBN 978-3-8382-0127-6

118 Jana Podßuweit
     Estlands Außen- und Sicherheitspolitik II
     Handlungsoptionen eines Kleinstaates im
     Rahmen seiner EU-Mitgliedschaft (2004-2008)
     Mit einem Vorwort von Helmut Hubel
     ISBN 978-3-8382-0440-6

119 Karin Pointner
     Estlands Außen- und Sicherheitspolitik III
     Eine gedächtnispolitische Analyse estnischer
     Entwicklungskooperation 2006-2010
     Mit einem Vorwort von Karin Liebhart
     ISBN 978-3-8382-0435-2

120 Ruslana Vovk
     Die Offenheit der ukrainischen
     Verfassung für das Völkerrecht und
     die europäische Integration
     Mit einem Vorwort von Alexander
     Blankenagel
     ISBN 978-3-8382-0481-9

121 Mykhaylo Banakh
     Die Relevanz der Zivilgesellschaft
     bei den postkommunistischen
     Transformationsprozessen in mittel-
     und osteuropäischen Ländern
     Das Beispiel der spät- und postsowjetischen
     Ukraine 1986-2009
     Mit einem Vorwort von Gerhard Simon
     ISBN 978-3-8382-0499-4

122 Michael Moser
     Language Policy and the Discourse on
     Languages in Ukraine under President
     Viktor Yanukovych (25 February
     2010–28 October 2012)
     ISBN 978-3-8382-0497-0 (Paperback edition)
     ISBN 978-3-8382-0507-6 (Hardcover edition)

123 Nicole Krome
     Russischer Netzwerkkapitalismus
     Restrukturierungsprozesse in der
     Russischen Föderation am Beispiel des
     Luftfahrtunternehmens "Aviastar"
     Mit einem Vorwort von Petra Stykow
     ISBN 978-3-8382-0534-2

124 David R. Marples
     'Our Glorious Past'
     Lukashenka's Belarus and
     the Great Patriotic War
     ISBN 978-3-8382-0574-8 (Paperback edition)
     ISBN 978-3-8382-0675-2 (Hardcover edition)

125 Ulf Walther
     Russlands "neuer Adel"
     Die Macht des Geheimdienstes von
     Gorbatschow bis Putin
     Mit einem Vorwort von Hans-Georg Wieck
     ISBN 978-3-8382-0584-7

126 Simon Geissbühler (Hrsg.)
     Kiew – Revolution 3.0
     Der Euromaidan 2013/14 und die
     Zukunftsperspektiven der Ukraine
     ISBN 978-3-8382-0581-6 (Paperback edition)
     ISBN 978-3-8382-0681-3 (Hardcover edition)

127 Andrey Makarychev
     Russia and the EU
     in a Multipolar World
     Discourses, Identities, Norms
     With a foreword by Klaus Segbers
     ISBN 978-3-8382-0629-5

128 Roland Scharff
     Kasachstan als postsowjetischer
     Wohlfahrtsstaat
     Die Transformation des sozialen
     Schutzsystems
     Mit einem Vorwort von Joachim Ahrens
     ISBN 978-3-8382-0622-6

129 Katja Grupp
     Bild Lücke Deutschland
     Kaliningrader Studierende sprechen über
     Deutschland
     Mit einem Vorwort von Martin Schulz
     ISBN 978-3-8382-0552-6

130 Konstantin Sheiko, Stephen Brown
     History as Therapy
     Alternative History and Nationalist
     Imaginings in Russia, 1991-2014
     ISBN 978-3-8382-0665-3

131 *Elisa Kriza*
Alexander Solzhenitsyn: Cold War Icon, Gulag Author, Russian Nationalist?
A Study of the Western Reception of his Literary Writings, Historical Interpretations, and Political Ideas
With a foreword by Andrei Rogatchevski
ISBN 978-3-8382-0589-2 (Paperback edition)
ISBN 978-3-8382-0690-5 (Hardcover edition)

132 *Serghei Golunov*
The Elephant in the Room
Corruption and Cheating in Russian Universities
ISBN 978-3-8382-0570-0

133 *Manja Hussner, Rainer Arnold (Hgg.)*
Verfassungsgerichtsbarkeit in Zentralasien I
Sammlung von Verfassungstexten
ISBN 978-3-8382-0595-3

134 *Nikolay Mitrokhin*
Die "Russische Partei"
Die Bewegung der russischen Nationalisten in der UdSSR 1953-1985
Aus dem Russischen übertragen von einem Übersetzerteam unter der Leitung von Larisa Schippel
ISBN 978-3-8382-0024-8

135 *Manja Hussner, Rainer Arnold (Hgg.)*
Verfassungsgerichtsbarkeit in Zentralasien II
Sammlung von Verfassungstexten
ISBN 978-3-8382-0597-7

136 *Manfred Zeller*
Das sowjetische Fieber
Fußballfans im poststalinistischen Vielvölkerreich
Mit einem Vorwort von Nikolaus Katzer
ISBN 978-3-8382-0757-5

137 *Kristin Schreiter*
Stellung und Entwicklungspotential zivilgesellschaftlicher Gruppen in Russland
Menschenrechtsorganisationen im Vergleich
ISBN 978-3-8382-0673-8

138 *David R. Marples, Frederick V. Mills (Eds.)*
Ukraine's Euromaidan
Analyses of a Civil Revolution
ISBN 978-3-8382-0660-8

139 *Bernd Kappenberg*
Setting Signs for Europe
Why Diacritics Matter for European Integration
With a foreword by Peter Schlobinski
ISBN 978-3-8382-0663-9

140 *René Lenz*
Internationalisierung, Kooperation und Transfer
Externe bildungspolitische Akteure in der Russischen Föderation
Mit einem Vorwort von Frank Ettrich
ISBN 978-3-8382-0751-3

141 *Juri Plusnin, Yana Zausaeva, Natalia Zhidkevich, Artemy Pozanenko*
Wandering Workers
Mores, Behavior, Way of Life, and Political Status of Domestic Russian Labor Migrants
Translated by Julia Kazantseva
ISBN 978-3-8382-0653-0

142 *Matthew Kott, David J. Smith (eds.)*
Latvia – A Work in Progress?
100 Years of State- and Nation-building
ISBN 978-3-8382-0648-6

143 *Инна Чувычкина (ред.)*
Экспортные нефте- и газопроводы на постсоветском пространстве
Анализ трубопроводной политики в свете теории международных отношений
ISBN 978-3-8382-0822-0

144 *Johann Zajaczkowski*
Russland – eine pragmatische Großmacht?
Eine rollentheoretische Untersuchung russischer Außenpolitik am Beispiel der Zusammenarbeit mit den USA nach 9/11 und des Georgienkrieges von 2008
Mit einem Vorwort von Siegfried Schieder
ISBN 978-3-8382-0837-4

145 *Boris Popivanov*
Changing Images of the Left in Bulgaria
The Challenge of Post-Communism in the Early 21st Century
ISBN 978-3-8382-0667-7

146 Lenka Krátká
       A History of the Czechoslovak Ocean
       Shipping Company 1948-1989
       How a Small, Landlocked Country Ran
       Maritime Business During the Cold War
       ISBN 978-3-8382-0666-0

147 Alexander Sergunin
       Explaining Russian Foreign Policy
       Behavior
       Theory and Practice
       ISBN 978-3-8382-0752-0

148 Darya Malyutina
       Migrant Friendships in
       a Super-Diverse City
       Russian-Speakers and their Social
       Relationships in London in the 21st Century
       With a foreword by Claire Dwyer
       ISBN 978-3-8382-0652-3

ibidem-Verlag

Melchiorstr. 15

D-70439 Stuttgart

info@ibidem-verlag.de

www.ibidem-verlag.de
www.ibidem.eu
www.edition-noema.de
www.autorenbetreuung.de